GOD'S FINAL EFFORT

by
John M. Haffert

LAF
PO Box 50
Asbury, NJ 08802

Nihil Obstat

In keeping with the decree of the Congregation for the Propagation of the Faith, A.A.S., 58, 1186, the publishers have exercised due care that there is nothing herein contrary to faith or morals and further declare that in all matters, and in all reference to alleged miracles or private revelations, they submit to the final and official judgment of the Magisterium of the Church.

"It is very necessary that this outstanding work be articulated to the Eucharistic and Marian faithful worldwide."

–Dr. Mark I. Miravalle, S.T.D.
International President of *Vox Populi Mediatrici*
Professor of Theology and Mariology at the Franciscan
University of Steubenville

Distributed in the U.S.A. by:
The 101 Foundation, Inc.
P.O. Box 151
Asbury, NJ 08802

Phone: (908) 689-8792
Fax: (908) 689-1957
www.101foundation.com
e-mail: 101@101foundation.com

ISBN: 1-890137-41-3

CONTENTS

FOREWORD

It was on May 2, 1999, the day of the beatification of Bl. Padre Pio, that I began to write this book as I asked myself the question:

With all the evil in the world, and so little interest in Fatima, is the Blue Army, of which Bl. Padre Pio was the spiritual father, no longer needed?

I was asking the question not only because of the decline in interest in Fatima but because of adversities in the apostolate itself (as described in *The Day I Didn't Die).*

If I am not mistaken, Bl. Padre Pio had me ask another question:

"If Sister Lucia says that the Fatima week has just begun, has not the world apostolate just begun?"

Immediately the thought came: "Look *at Fatima in the context of history."* And there flooded to my mind how the atom bomb and the miracle of Fatima placed us at the hinge of history, with the threat of nuclear destruction countered by the promise of triumph. Then the thought came:

"What did Sister Lucia mean by the *week* of Fatima, and what was the meaning of the words of Our Lord when He told Sister Lucia that our failure to respond to the requests of Fatima was like the failed response to the "final effort" of His Sacred Heart?

With those thoughts, and invoking Bl. Padre Pio who seems to have inspired them, this book was begun.

Numerous faces of persons with whom I was intimately involved in Fatima Apostolate have come up before me in addition to Bl. Padre Pio: Bishop da Silva and Bishop Venancio (the first two bishops of Fatima), Abbé André Richard of Paris, Albert Setz Degen in Switzerland, Msgr. Strazzacappa in Italy, Msgr. Colgan, Hon. Henrietta Bowers from England, Father Fuhs from Germany, a host of others.

Now they are all gone from this world. Perhaps I have survived so that I might write this book. I beg their prayers, not so much for me but for the writing and for the world for which this message is vitally important.

Sister Lucia as the author saw her on May 31, 1999, day of the golden jubilee of her profession as a Carmelite nun.

The author had just published his book *Too Late?* based on the startling messages given by Sister Lucia in October, 1993, in which she said an atomic war had been avoided in 1985, and that we are now in the "third day of the Fatima week."

The world had gained time.

This sequel to *Too Late?* sees "the final effort to wrest mankind from the reign of Satan" (first revealed to St. Margaret Mary Alacoque) as now deadlining to a conclusion.

Dedicated to my sister,
Sister Therese of the Queen of Carmel, D.C.,
my spiritual life partner, as she enters her
80th year, August 10, 1999

CHAPTER ONE

TERRIBLY SERIOUS

As billions of people entered the new millennium, the still-living visionary of Fatima, Sister Lucia, had just said (on October 11, 1993) something of startling importance— something vital to every living man, woman, and child. And only a few knew it.

In the got-to-the-moon century in which history somersaulted at the destruction of Hiroshima, she had seen the Mother of God.

What she saw and heard was confirmed by one of the most amazing miracles in history. It was justly called "the greatest event since Pentecost." It was God's intervention to prepare for the moment when, as Pope John Paul II expressed it, man had arrived at the alternative of self-destruction.

To understand the importance of what she said on October 11, 1993, one must see it in the perspective of that frightening alternative.

The atomic destruction of Hiroshima became what Jean Guitton calls *"the hinge of history,"* and **the event of Fatima is *the spiritual side of that hinge.***

Now, at the end of the got-to-the moon century, *God's messenger to the atomic age* had just made a haunting statement for the people of the new millennium.

Not Changed by the Years

I saw Sister Lucia at some length in the intimacy of the parlor of her convent in Coimbra, Portugal, on May 31, 1999. I was pleased to see her smile because she had not had too much to smile about in previous years. She had received six terrible prophecies from the Blessed Virgin Mary, beginning May 13, 1917. She had seen five of those prophecies, one by one, come true. And she had sorrowed that the world had not listened.

The first time I had seen her, in an interview which lasted over three hours, she had never smiled. She was explaining what was necessary to prevent atomic war and to bring about the era of peace promised by Our Lady of Fatima.[1]

It was terribly serious.

The next time I saw her (1952), there was at least a glimmer of a smile. The message was becoming known.

When I saw her on May 31, 1999, she was smiling from the time she came into the room almost until she left. It was the fiftieth anniversary of her profession as a Carmelite nun. She could smile not just because of the joy of a family visit for her golden jubilee but because recent word from Rome indicated that the Church and the world would have fresh confirmation that the Fatima message was indeed from Heaven: The Pope had decided to beatify the two children who had shared the Fatima event with her.[2]

"An Ongoing Process"

As the world was entering the new millennium on the tidal wave of a century of wars and evil unprecedented in history, in an interview with Cardinal Vidal on October 11, 1993, she said: "People expect things to happen immediately within their own time frame. But Fatima is still in its third day. *The triumph is an ongoing process.*"

Then, repeating herself, she said: "Fatima is still in its third day. We are now in the post consecration period. The first day was the apparition period. The second was the post apparition, pre-consecration period. *The Fatima week has not yet ended.*"

---

[1] This interview took place in July, 1947, and resulted in the founding of the Blue Army.

[2] This is the step before canonization for which a miracle was required. It declares that the children practiced heroic virtue and are now in Heaven.

"I may not get to see the whole week..." Then she repeated: "*The Fatima week has just begun.* How can one expect it to be over immediately?"

St. Margaret Mary certainly did not get to see the whole week of response to the messages she received from the Sacred Heart. Perhaps the following dates will help the reader understand.

	1st Day	*2nd Day*	*3rd Day*
Sacred Heart	1673–1689	1689–1899	1899–1917
Immaculate Heart	1916–1929	1929–1984	1984–

In Sister Lucia's imagery, the first day is the apparition period; the second day is the post apparition, pre-consecration period; the third day is from the consecration onwards.

The third day of the final appeal of the Sacred Heart came to a climax in 1917 with the atheist revolution in Russia and two world wars, culminating in the use of the atomic bomb.

How will the third day of the "Fatima week" end?

The Rest of the Week?

Given at the dawn of the new millennium, this message from Sister Lucia had an importance deeper and more urgent than at first perceived. She herself seems to have felt this. *She had carefully prepared what she was going to say and had waited up for hours on the night of October 11, 1993 for the arrival of a Cardinal of the Church who would make it known.*[3]

Under the auspices of this same Cardinal during the previous three years, I had been editing the magazine *Voice of the Sacred Hearts* to promote the message now emphasized in this book.

The Cardinal discussed this with her. He asked if it fulfilled Our Lady's requests. Her answer made clear that the third day of Fatima concerns the will of Our Lord that devotion to the Immaculate Heart of His Mother be related to devotion to His Own Sacred Heart.

---

[3] The Cardinal was delayed and the interview took place at eleven o'clock at night, long after this elderly nun's bedtime.

Particularly haunting is what she did *not* say. Although she described the first three days, *what are the other days which remain?*

Sister Lucia's historic October 11, 1993 interview with His Eminence, Ricardo Cardinal Vidal.

Chapter Two

THE THIRD DAY

In the message of Fatima, the change in Russia was promised only if the Pope, together with all the bishops of the world, would consecrate that nation to the Immaculate Heart of Mary.

What was overlooked, and is still alarmingly ignored, is that when one Pope after another failed to make this collegial consecration of Russia, Lucia asked Our Lord, on the command of her confessor, why He insisted on this consecration. Our Lord answered:

"Because I want the entire Church to know that this favor (the change in Russia) was obtained *through the Immaculate Heart of My Mother,* so that *afterwards, it may extend this devotion of the Five First Saturdays and place devotion to Her Immaculate Heart alongside devotion to My Own Sacred Heart."*

All Those Wars

Stop and think of all those wars of the last century! Think of the millions who died, not only in wars but in the crushing advance of communism over a third of the world, making it the bloodiest century in history.

Yet the first thing Sister Lucia said in that 1993 message was that "ALL THE WARS COULD HAVE BEEN AVOIDED," if the requests had been heard.

Indeed, when the collegial consecration was finally made on March 25, 1984, the change in Russia followed within months (as we have documented elsewhere) and became fully apparent with the dissolution of the Soviet Union six years later.

Third Day Began

In that same interview in October of 1993 (which was recorded on both audio and video tape and therefore is completely accurate), Sister Lucia explained that the collegial consecration made on March 25, 1984 was accepted by God. She said that the "conversion" of Russia, which meant the granting of freedom of religion in that country, *was brought about by God* and brought us into the "third day."

We presume the seventh day will be the "era of peace" promised by Our Lady in the words: *"Finally my Immaculate Heart will triumph, and an era of peace will be granted to mankind."*

What will the fourth day bring? And the fifth and sixth? Could the fourth be the time of the warning and purification? Fifth the time of the remnant (pre-triumph)? Sixth the time of the triumph leading into the era of peace?

Even more important: *What is expected of us now, in this third day?*

Communions of Reparation

In a letter to her confessor on May 29, 1930, Sister Lucia repeated that Our Lord promised the change in Russia when the collegial consecration was made. Next, Our Lord said:

"The Holy Father must then promise that upon the ending of this persecution (of religion in Russia), *he will approve and recommend the practice of the reparatory devotion* (i.e. the Five First Saturdays)."

So now, following the change in Russia, is the time when the Holy Father is to approve and promote the First Saturday devotion. It is the "day" when whatever happens next in this unfolding Divine saga will depend on how many respond to the basic requests of Fatima and the Communions of Reparation.

This seems to place the *weight of responsibility for the entire world* on Catholics. They alone are able to make Communions of Reparation. But it is possible for all (eminently including Muslims[4]) to recognize the role of Mary as the Immaculate new Eve.

In the face of this responsibility, is it not frightening that so few seem even to know?

This present book *God's Final Effort* is a sequel to *Too Late?* (shown above), which is based on events in Rwanda and the Balkans, where it became "too late" (see inside back cover).

---

[4] Muslims believe in the Immaculate Conception and the Virgin birth. Prince Pahlavi, successor to the Shah of Iran, wrote a book on Fatima (the daughter of Mohammed) in which he said that the Virgin Mary could be a bridge between Muslims and Christians. See the author's book *Too Late?*.

Chapter Three

REQUIREMENT OF THE THIRD DAY

The burning question of the moment must be: *Is the requirement of Our Lord for this "third day" being fulfilled?*

Our Lord Himself clearly explained that requirement. He said that after the consecration, and after the change in Russia (which He would then bring about), *devotion to the Immaculate Heart of His Mother was to be placed alongside devotion to His Own Sacred Heart, especially by means of the First Saturday Communions of Reparation.*

As I said in my last book *Too Late?*, most do not seem to realize the gravity of this. Most lay persons feel it is not up to them, but up to "the Church," as though they were not a responsible part of the Church.

Some say: Why doesn't the Pope cry out to the world that it must listen?

He has cried out in word and deed.

Strong Message of the Pope

Pope John Paul II, who week after week led the First Saturday Rosary in the company of thousands and on radio and TV, said in his special letter to Fatima on October 13, 1997, *Fatima is one of the greatest signs of our time* not so much because of the miracle but because it *shows us the alternative*, and tells us the *specific response* needed to meet that alternative: To choose peace or self-destruction!

Those are the words of the Pope: "Greatest signs of our time...specific response...the alternative...to save mankind from self-destruction."

As we have said, the Pope has for years personally lead the Rosary in the presence of thousands and on radio and television every First Saturday.

The question is not what is the Pope doing. The question is what am *I doing* to make the Pope's voice *heard?*

Popes Anticipated Our Lady

In that October 13, 1997 letter, the Pope explained the reason for it all. He said Our Lady of Fatima came with *specific requests "to save mankind from itself."*

Those specific requests call for national and personal consecration to the Immaculate Heart of Mary[5] and for Communions of Reparation on the First Saturday of five consecutive months. And, this devotion was established *before* the Fatima apparitions.

Pope John Paul XII praying at the place of the apparitions of Our Lady of Fatima. He said these apparitions are one of the greatest signs of our time because they offer the specific response needed to save mankind from self-destruction.

Two Popes, one after the other, anticipated this request from Heaven. The devotion was instituted by the Church *before* Our Lady indicated that it was part of God's "final effort."

The First Saturday Devotion of Reparation to the Immaculate Heart was introduced, in 1904, by St. Pius X. The same Pope granted additional indulgences to encourage it on June 13, 1912.

Five years later, on that same day (June 13), in the second apparition of Fatima, Our Lady told Lucia she was to remain in the world because "Jesus wishes to use you to make me known and loved. *He wishes to establish in the world devotion to my Immaculate Heart.*"

On July 13th, in the third apparition of Fatima, Our Lady said She would ask for the First Saturday Communions of Reparation. This She did on December 10, 1925. Again, five years *before* (November 13, 1920) the Church, in the person of Pope Benedict XV, had encouraged the First Saturday devotion established by St. Pius X with still further indulgences.

This action of the Church, *before and therefore completely independent of the apparitions*, was also evident in the revelations of the Sacred Heart.

Warning and Promise

In this message of the First Saturday devotion, the two dates of July 13, 1917, and December 10, 1925, stand out because of a warning and a promise:

On July 13, 1917, Our Lady prophesied "**annihilation of several entire nations**" and then said: "*To prevent this I shall come to ask for consecration of Russia to my*

---

[5] A simple act of consecration, a "placing of one's name in Our Lady's maternal Heart," is a beginning. But to be consecrated to the Immaculate Heart, in fact, requires purity of life. It requires making the sacrifices required to keep God's commandments. And Our Lady holds out to us the Scapular (which Pius XII called "our sign of consecration") and the Rosary to help us. For further details, see especially the author's books *Sign of Her Heart, To Prevent This,* and *Her Glorious Title.*

Immaculate Heart, and for First Saturday Communions of Reparation."

On December 10, 1925, when She came to request these First Saturday Communions of Reparation, She made a great promise for all those who would complete the five consecutively: "*I will assist them at the hour of death with all the graces necessary...*"

Great Incentive

The value of an act is often measured by its reward. So is its importance. And the reward for this devotion of Communions of Reparation is great almost beyond understanding.

The Queen of Heaven will prevent atomic war if we do as She asks, and She promises at the hour of death "all the graces necessary" to those who respond.

Her Divine Son had already promised the graces necessary for salvation for those who complete nine consecutive Communions of Reparation on First Fridays. And we have reason to believe that "*all* the graces necessary" include the grace of a *peaceful* death—the ultimate grace of joyful transition to our eternal reward.

Most people fear death so much they try never to think about it. Many in the face of death are seized with fear. It is the ultimate, decisive point in the lives of each of us. All the treasures and honors of the world are, in that moment, nothing.

At that dreaded and critical moment, the greatest possible gift, exceeding every other possible gift in this world (other than the Sacraments themselves), is what Our Lady is promising to those who fulfill Her simple request.

Is it not almost unbelievable that, even with so great an incentive as this, and despite the looming threat of atomic destruction to be avoided if enough persons embrace this same devotion, this awesome message from Heaven is widely ignored?

Chapter Four

TOO LATE

It is of utmost importance to see the link between the change in Russia and the First Saturday devotion.

They are first linked by Our Lady in the words: "To prevent this (the annihilation of nations) I shall come to ask for the consecration of Russia to my Immaculate Heart, and for the First Saturday Communions of Reparation."

Next they were linked by Our Lord when He explained that He insisted on the collegial consecration of Russia to the Immaculate Heart of His Mother, so that afterwards[6] (after the consecration and the subsequent change in Russia), devotion to Her Immaculate Heart would be placed alongside devotion to His Own Sacred Heart and **then the Pope would propagate and encourage the First Saturday devotion.**

It follows, as we have said before, that this is the time (the third day, the post-consecration period) for what Pope John Paul II has called *"the alliance of the Two Hearts,"* and for the Communions of Reparation.

Important Parallel

It is also important to see the parallel in history between the way the world ignored the requests of Heaven for devotion to the Sacred Heart, and the way it has ignored the request to place devotion to the Immaculate Heart of Mary "alongside devotion to My Own Sacred Heart."

---

[6] Our Lord had promised that when the collegial consecration was made, the change in Russia would take place. So this refers to the time after the conseration and the change in Russia.

Our Lord Himself, in one of His colloquies with Sister Lucia, referred to this parallel between how the world reacted to the revelations of His Sacred Heart to St. Margaret Mary Alacoque, and how the world has reacted (and is reacting right now) to the request for devotion to the Immaculate Heart of His Mother.

On August 29, 1931, Our Lord told Sister Lucia: "*Make known to My ministers that given the example of the King of France in not executing My command, they will in turn fall into misfortune.*"

Does this mean that Popes and Bishops will suffer as happened in France? When the grandson of Louis XIV was beheaded, so were 2,400 bishops, priests, and nuns. And, commenting on the words of Our Lord quoted above, Sister Lucia said:

"Unless this act intervenes (the consecration to the Immaculate Heart), war will end (in the world) only when the blood spilled by the martyrs is enough to appease Divine Justice."

The lessons to be drawn from this comparison, made by Our Lord Himself, will be revealed in the paragraphs which follow. Behind it all is the gradual unfolding of the meaning of the gospels through the years.

Unfolding Doctrine

Devotion to the Sacred Heart began early in the Church. Notably in the 13th century when, on the feast of St. John the Evangelist, St. Gertrude had a vision in which St. John revealed the depth of devotion to the Sacred Heart which he experienced when he rested his head on the Heart of Jesus at the last supper.

She asked St. John why he had not mentioned this in his gospel.

The evangelist explained that this has been an "unfolding" message—only *later coming into focus.* He told St. Gertrude: "*My writings were for the Church in its infancy.*"

The Church has been maturing for 2,000 years. Late in that maturation is our ability to grasp the role of the Sacred Hearts of Jesus and Mary in the economy of salvation.

The Historic Parallel

In 1673, over four hundred years after the apparition of St. John to St. Gertrude, three hundred years before the new millennium 2000, Jesus revealed His Sacred Heart to St. Margaret Mary. He made eight amazing promises to those who would practice this devotion, the greatest of which was: Those who would make a Communion of Reparation to His Sacred Heart on nine consecutive First Fridays would not go to Hell.[7]

The saint was told that God desired this devotion to the Heart of Jesus because His Heart had suffered so much for our salvation.

This, of course, is why He desires devotion to the Immaculate Heart of His Mother, which Simeon foresaw would be "pierced by a sword." Her heart suffered with His.

Both devotions, unfolding one after the other, are in a way "final."

---

[7] This does not imply that even a person in mortal sin could be saved. It means that a person who has worthily made the nine Friday communions of reparation to the Sacred Heart will die in the state of Grace.

Triumph

St. Margaret Mary said that Jesus revealed to Her that this was a *"final effort of His Love to favor human beings in the last centuries of the world, and to withdraw them from the empire of Satan, which He intends to destroy and to replace with the reign of His Love."*

We presume that when Our Lord said this final effort was being made "in the last centuries of the world" that those centuries began at the time He spoke. Since then, already more than three centuries have passed.

But here we are not preoccupied with time but with the spiritual crisis of here and now.

Our Lord told St. Margaret Mary that Satan greatly fears this devotion and would *do everything to hinder it*, "knowing how many souls would, because of it, be converted and sanctified."

Our Lady at Fatima said that finally Her Immaculate Heart *would triumph*. And Jesus had said He would *reign through His Heart, despite His enemies.* By the "Alliance of the Two Hearts," we are approaching the triumph. And again the Church takes the lead. Two symposiums of world-class theologians, directly under the auspices of the Pope, have presented the solid theological foundations for that expression which Pope John Paul II had repeatedly used: "The Alliance of the Two Hearts."[8]

The consequences of continuing to ignore this final effort of God's Love could be catastrophic.

A Frightening Discovery

As we continue to look at the historic parallel between the lack of response to the revelations of the Sacred Heart and those of the Immaculate Heart (as Jesus did in His words to Sister Lucia), we come to a frightening discovery.

The revelations of the First Saturdays in 1925 were followed in 1930 with an explanation of their important connection *to the consecration of Russia, which had*

---

[8] See *Theology of the Alliance of the Two Hearts*, published by AHFI, Box 1719, Dover, DE 19903.

embraced militant atheism and spread its errors throughout the world. The revelations of the Sacred Heart (which took place between 1673 and 1676) were followed in 1689 by a request for the *consecration to the Sacred Heart of the nation of France, from which the atheistic revolution would rise.*

We see, therefore, that *long before it happened, the God of history was offering His Love to prevent the miseries which man was about to bring upon himself.*

He made His appeal of Love when the atheistic revolution was first brewing in France.

A hundred years later, it would be too late for France. *Before how many years will it be too late for us?*

His Promises Rejected

Jesus told St. Margaret Mary: "The eternal Father, wishing to repair the bitterness and agony which the Heart of Jesus endured in the palaces of earthly princes, wishes to make use of the reigning monarch of France (Louis XIV) to proclaim public devotion of reparation to that Sacred Heart." He asked that the king erect a shrine in which a picture of his Divine Heart would receive homage, and that the king request the Holy See to authorize the Mass in honor of the Sacred Heart. He said:

"It is by this Divine Heart that God wishes to dispense the treasures of His graces and of salvation."

In return, Our Lord promised that the king would be the friend of His Sacred Heart, and would have His *blessing and protection from all his enemies.*

But the French court was rife with scandal. Louis XIV had another love he was not willing to give up for the Love of Jesus. He did not respond to the request of the Sacred Heart even though knowledge of this extraordinary message appeared to have spread in the court, some of whose ladies began to practice the devotion.

Let us take note of this. Just as since 1984 all the bishops of the entire world know the message of the Immaculate

Heart, the king of France *knew* the message of the Sacred Heart. (We will refer later to this important parallel.)

Not for Lack of Knowing!

In the light of history, it is somewhat amazing that Louis XIV did not respond. In 1667, the first series of wars began which continued throughout his entire reign. Yet Our Lord was promising to end the wars and give great graces and benefits: "Success to his armies, so as to make him triumphant over the malice of his enemies."

Nine years after the King refused to accept the devotion, in a second war against the Netherlands, France was defeated. Then came the war of the Spanish Succession, in which France was defeated again. Finally, impoverished by war, the nation fell into a state of economic crisis which ended in the debacle of the French revolution.

All this failed to move the spiritually lukewarm king. His son, Louis XV, also did not respond. *And exactly 100 years after the Sacred Heart made His ignored request, in 1789 came the French revolution which destroyed the monarchy and set the stage for worldwide disasters.*[9]

---

[9] St. Margaret Mary said that the rejection of Our Lord's "final effort" was "*a sword that pierced my heart with deep grief.*" One must think also of the suffering of Sister Lucia during the sixty-seven years before the "third day" of the Fatima week.

CHAPTER FIVE

OUR BELATED EFFORT

Cast by the leaders of the French revolution into the Bastille prison, the grandson of the king who had received the request of the Sacred Heart was awaiting execution. Was it too late? Even though the requests had been ignored for a hundred years, if he did finally what God had asked of his grandfather, would the Sacred Heart give him protection?

A document on which was recorded the last will and testament of the desperate monarch was found wedged in the wall of the prison. It read:

"If God will deliver me from this prison alive within a year, with the bishops of my Kingdom, I will take all necessary measures to establish in canonical form a solemn feast in honor of the Sacred Heart of Jesus, to be celebrated in perpetuity throughout France on the Friday following the Octave of Corpus Christi. This shall be followed by a public procession to repair the outrages and profanations performed in the holy temples by schismatics, heretics, and bad Christians. Within three months I will go to Notre Dame,[10] and at the foot of the altar I will pronounce a solemn consecration of my person and of my kingdom to the Sacred Heart of Jesus, with a promise to give my subjects an example of the honor and love due to this Sacred Heart."

He postscribed a further promise: "Every year I shall renew the act of consecration with procession."

---

[10] The cathedral of Paris in which all the French kings since the 13th century had been crowned.

Cut off from his people by the walls of his prison, he could make this promise only to the prison walls. But, he wrote that he was "ready to do so also in my blood," and added: "The most beautiful day of my life will be when I shall publish this aloud in all the churches of my realm."

But only prison walls could hear. *It was too late.*

Responsibility Now

God placed the responsibility for responding to the requests of the Sacred Heart upon the king of France and the French nation.

In the case of the revelations of the Immaculate Heart, God placed the responsibility upon the bishops of the world and upon the Church.

Jesus "insisted" that *all the bishops of the world* be informed and participate so that "*My entire Church* will know...so that *it may extend this devotion later on, and put this devotion alongside devotion to my Sacred Heart.*[11]" ("Later on" refers to the time after cessation of religious persecution in Russia, circa 1990.)

What was the role of the Pope in this?

Obviously it was up to the Pope to take the initiative. But he was not asked to act on his own as seems to have been the case of the king of France. Our Lord involved all the bishops of the world, and spoke of "My entire Church" in asking for the implementation of the First Saturday Devotion of Reparation.

Pope's Mission Like St. Claude's?

Might we conclude that as God chose St. Claude after St. Margaret Mary as the principal messenger for the revelations of the Sacred Heart, for the revelations of the Immaculate Heart, *after Sister Lucia, God chose the Pope himself?*

In *Crossing the Threshold of Hope*, the Pope affirmed that the Fatima message was from God. He said the children

---

[11] Letter of Sr. Lucia, May 18, 1936. In this statement, "later on" means after the change in Russia. See *Her Own Words to the Nuclear Age* by Haffert, pg. 306.

of Fatima "could not have invented those predictions," and added:

"Perhaps this is also why the Pope was called from a faraway country, perhaps this is why it was necessary for the assassination attempt to be made in St. Peter's Square precisely on May 13, 1981, the anniversary of the first apparition of Fatima—so that all could become more transparent and comprehensible, *so that the voice of God which speaks in human history* through the signs of the times *could be more easily heard and understood."* (Emphasis added.)[12]

John Paul II was rudely awakened to study the Fatima message by an assassin's bullet in St. Peter's Square on May 13, 1981, feast of Our Lady of Fatima. *The bullet also struck the Pope into a new awareness of Fatima as he himself said.*

From his hospital bed the Pontiff sent for all the documents of Fatima, which he now had time to study carefully.

Instructions Sent to All Bishops

Finally realizing the urgency and importance of the Fatima message, he decided to send letters of instruction,

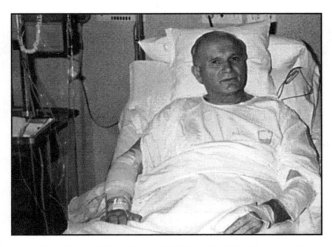

Pope John Paul II in Gemelli Hospital in Rome. During his three months of recovery, he studied the documents of Fatima.

transcribed in their own languages (rather than in Latin or in just a few common languages), to every bishop in the world. Included were detailed acts of consecration of the world and of Russia to the Immaculate Heart of Mary.

Less than eight months after emerging from the hospital, the Pope went in person to Fatima (May 13, 1982) to make the consecration.

Apparently not all the bishops of the world responded. Perhaps, in his haste, the Pope had not made clear that he was renewing the two acts of the consecration of Russia and the world, previously made by Pius XII, and that he asked all the bishops to JOIN with him in that act.

So another letter went out to the more than two thousand bishops of the world that they might participate with the Pope, who would make the consecration again, this time in St. Peter's Square (March 25, 1984).

Still To Be Done!

The request for the collegial consecration to the Immaculate Heart of Mary was fulfilled.[13]

But the reparatory devotion to Her Immaculate Heart, which Our Lord asked to be promoted throughout the Church following the act of consecration, is still largely ignored.

And is that not the most important part of what God requires to save the world from atomic war?

After prophesying that "several entire nations will be annihilated," Our Lady said that "*to prevent this,* I shall come to ask for the consecration of Russia to My Immaculate Heart (which had now been done) *and for the First Saturday Communions of Reparation.*"

---

[12] *Crossing the Threshold of Hope*, pg. 131.

[13] There are some who deny this because the Pope did not explicitly mention Russia in the act of consecration. They ignore that all the bishops of the world had been sent the entire document of the consecration of Russia made by Pius XII in 1954, which John Paul II was now renewing in union with all the world's bishops. Sister Lucia said positively that this was accepted by God.

Our Lord had promised that when the collegial conse-cration was made, there would be a change in Russia with cessation of religious persecution in that country. The reason He "insisted" on the collegial consecration was so that afterwards, "*My entire Church will know that it was through the Immaculate Heart of My Mother that this favor was obtained*, so that later on it may extend this devotion..."

Incredible as it seems, it appears that after all those years of wars and suffering and *almost daily threat of nuclear war*, God abruptly brought about the change in Russia just so all the bishops of the world would know beyond doubt that they had to promote devotion of reparation to the Immaculate Heart of Mary.

In fact, of course, the change in Russia and the end of the cold war could have come much sooner if the collegial consecration had come sooner. Sister Lucia was told that *it was **because of the world's failure** to respond to the message of Fatima that the Popes were not moved to make the collegial consecration sooner.*[14]

In a word, we are *all* responsible.

Our Lord said explicitly to Sister Lucia that the consecration was delayed because we had not *deserved* it.

In a letter of August 18, 1940, Sister Lucia explained the delay: "*To punish the world with His Justice for so many crimes* and to prepare it for a more complete turn towards Him."

Are we finally "prepared" to accept the message? Will the next Divine Intervention, whatever it may be, turn the tide?

Only if we, and in particular the laity, vigorously intervene.

It is so easy, and self-excusing, to place the responsibility on the shoulders of the Pope and the bishops. In fact, an entire book could be written on all that the Popes have done to call the attention of the world to the Fatima message.

---

[14] *Her Own Words to the Nuclear Age*, by Haffert, pg. 307.

The Popes Have Acted

Pope Pius XII consecrated the world to the Immaculate Heart.

Pope John XXIII instituted the Feast of Our Lady of Fatima.

Pope Paul VI made an unprecedented trip to Fatima (at a time when Popes rarely left the Vatican) and affirmed the message before the entire world.

Pope John Paul II made the collegial consecration and has honored the Immaculate Heart of Mary alongside devotion to the Sacred Heart in many ways, even speaking of the "alliance of the Two Hearts."

Rome has made the feast of Her Immaculate Heart obligatory and placed it on the day after the feast of the Sacred Heart (which falls on the Friday following the octave of Corpus Christi), thus liturgically relating the Sacred Heart and the Eucharist and the Two Hearts of Jesus and Mary.

Since the Popes have responded in this manner, and since all the bishops of the world responded by participating in the collegial consecration of March 25, 1984, what response is needed now?

Pope Paul VI "presents" Sister Lucia to a crowd of hundreds of thousands at Fatima on May 13, 1967, and to other millions by television, as though to say: "Here is Our Lady's messenger."

As we shall see in a moment, *what finally happened with fulfillment of the requests of the Sacred Heart reveals that a special and very important* **responsibility lies on the shoulders of the laity.**

A Bitter Lesson

Our Lord Himself had told Sister Lucia that as the kings of France had ignored the requests of His Sacred Heart, these requests in favor of the Heart of His Mother would finally be fulfilled...**"too late."**

The exact words of Our Lord were: "They will repent and do it, but it will be too late. Russia will already have spread her errors throughout the world provoking wars and persecution of the Church. The Holy Father will have much to suffer."[15]

It was in saying this that Our Lord compared *our belated reaction* to the revelations of the Immaculate Heart, to the belated reaction of the kings of France to those of His Sacred Heart.

The comparison becomes a bitter lesson indeed when we recall that before he wrote that document in the Bastille, while the gutters of Paris ran with blood, Louis XVI must have been previously *well informed* of all the requests of the Sacred Heart: for the *collegial consecration* of the nation (himself with all the bishops of the realm), for *the feast,* for the permanent *chapel* to the Sacred Heart, for *annual renewal of the consecration.* (How similar to all the requests for the Immaculate Heart!)

In the face of his execution by the mob, he desperately pledged them all. But one must wonder: *Why did he not make those simple acts before it was too late?*

And why do we now hesitate to fulfill the simple requests asked of us? What is missing? Who is responsible?

---

[15] *Her Own Words to the Nuclear Age*, by Haffert, pg. 308.

Chapter Six

IMPORTANCE OF THE CONSECRATIONS

After the last will and testament of Louis XVI was found wedged in the stones of his cell, and even after all the tragedies of France and the birth in Paris of worldwide atheism formalized in the writings of Karl Marx, France did not respond to the requests made to St. Margaret Mary *until two hundred years later*, when France was on the verge of being conquered in 1870 in the Franco–Prussian war.

Then, a group of lay persons came forward and petitioned the Archbishop of Paris to fulfill the requests of the Sacred Heart. At the same time, they offered to raise funds to build the requested chapel with an image of the Sacred Heart, and suggested it be on the hill above Paris (the hill on which early Christians had died for the faith).

Responding to this initiative, the Archbishop wrote to all the bishops of France asking their participation. France was consecrated to the Sacred Heart, and the "chapel" on Montmartre, with the image of the Sacred Heart and perpetual adoration of the Blessed Sacrament, became a magnificent Basilica that has become a landmark of the French capital.

Immediate Response from Heaven

Almost immediately after the laity had taken this initiative, Our Lady appeared in 1871 in the sky at Pontmain, a short distance from where the German armies, after overrunning most of France, had taken the city of Lavalle. In

Her hands was a blood red crucifix. A band appeared at Her feet with the words: "*Continue to pray. My son permits Himself (His Heart) to be touched.*"

At that same moment, Our Lady revealed Her Immaculate Heart in the church of Our Lady of Victories in Paris.[16] Forty-two stars appeared at Her feet, the war ended immediately, and there followed forty two years of peace.

Consecrations of the World

What had happened in France became a grace for the world.

In 1898, upon the heels of these events in France, Jesus appeared to a Good Shepherd nun, Mother Mary of the Divine Heart, in a convent on the outskirts of the city of Oporto, in Portugal. He asked that the Pope make the consecration of the world to His Sacred Heart.

In response, Pope Leo XIII wrote *Annum Sacrum* in 1899, opening the new century with a request for the consecration. The encyclical was sent *to all the Bishops of the world, commanding them to join in this world consecration to the Sacred Heart on June 11, 1899.*

Leo XIII had one of the longest and most fruitful reigns in the history of the papacy and he said that *this consecration* was "*the greatest act of my pontificate,*" from which "*I expect great graces for the world.*"

Why?

Perhaps many of us may have difficulty in seeing that an act of consecration could be so important.

Why did it take so long (until the dawn of *the last century* of the second millennium) to consecrate the world to the Sacred Heart? Why did it take so long (to the dawn of the *first century* of the new millennium) to consecrate the world to the Immaculate Heart of His Mother. Why?

---

[16] This is a story of great significance to the Immaculate Heart devotion. As a result, the first confraternity of the Immaculate Heart of Mary was founded. See the author's two books: *What Happened at Pontmain?* and *Finally, Russia.*

Out of many reasons, two in particular are suggested:

1) The world had to be *ready* for these acts to be made;

2) Mankind had to understand that the acts themselves are a renunciation of Satan, at the same time they are a consecration to God through those greatest signs of His Love: the Hearts of Jesus and Mary.

Our Lord Himself said that the reason the Pope was not moved to make the collegial consecration during almost eighty years was because **the world had not responded** to the message given at Fatima.

The Alternative

The world had not responded even though God had given the sign of a great miracle, witnessed by tens of thousands, "so that all may believe" that they had to mend their lives. Otherwise, they would suffer another world war, atheism would spread from Russia throughout the world fostering other wars, and so on. And they had either not believed, did not respond, or both.

So the consecration was delayed. All those tragedies happened before it was finally made, and the Soviet Union was dissolved.

So the first reason was OUR lack of response. And the second reason is self-evident. If I consecrate myself to the Sacred Heart, I will want to avoid what offends His Heart; if I am consecrated to the most pure Heart of Mary, I will want to avoid what offends that most pure Heart.

A prerequisite to the consecration was a sincere resolution, at least of a sufficient number persons, to avoid what would offend Their Hearts.

Must Be Renewed Annually

We are weak, and resolutions are easily broken. They have to be renewed.

Pope St. Pius X, in 1906, commanded *renewal* of the consecration to the Sacred Heart throughout the world. In 1925, Pope Pius XI made the renewal of the whole world and mandated that it be renewed annually on the Feast of Christ the King. And Pope Pius XII, who had consecrated the world to the Immaculate Heart of Mary on the occasion of the 25th anniversary of the apparitions of Fatima in 1942, now *commanded* twelve years later (1954) that this consecration to the Immaculate Heart be renewed annually on the Feast of Our Lady's Queenship.

Consecration to Their Hearts is a recognition of Their sovereign rights over us. Jesus is King by right and by conquest (as God and as Redeemer) and Mary is Queen by right and by conquest (as His Mother and as the Mother at the foot of Cross).

The commands of the vicars of Christ for annual renewal of consecration to Their Sacred Hearts have been largely ignored. *Perhaps this is one of the reasons the Fatima week advances so slowly.*

Sister Lucia speaks to Pope John Paul II at Fatima, May 13, 1982. His Holiness understood that further participation of the bishops of the world was needed for collegial consecration to obtain the promised changes in Russia. His Holiness was able to accomplish this on March 25, 1984. Now there is a call to **renew the consecration** throughout the world.

Now on One Day

It has been suggested that now the renewal of consecration to the Sacred Heart and to the Immaculate Heart be made on one day: the Sunday immediately following their feasts.[17]

The feast of the Sacred Heart is on Friday, and of the Immaculate Heart on the day following, which is of course Saturday. Since the next day is a Sunday, when all go to Mass, would it not be simple for the Church to have the act of consecration after all Masses on that day? Then the "entire Church," as Jesus requested, would be responding.[18]

Even if we do not understand the importance of the consecrations and of their regular, periodical renewal, we can believe the great promises which have been made by the Hearts of Jesus and Mary. They have used the words *protection, victory, triumph,* and *an era of peace for mankind.*

When Pope Leo XIII made the consecration to the Sacred Heart a hundred years ago, he said: "I expected from this consecration *the greatest graces for the whole world.*" And when Pope Pius XII mandated annual renewal of the consecration to the Immaculate Heart in 1954, he said: "*In this lies the world's greatest hope.*"

Thirty years later, in 1984, making the collegial consecration to the Immaculate Heart in Rome, in union with all the bishops of the world, Pope John Paul II expressed a similar hope. And, in his book *Crossing the Threshold of Hope*, he said: "***As we approach the millennium, the words of Our Lady of Fatima seem to be nearing their fulfillment.***"

So where are we in the *Fatima week?*

---

[17] Ven. Cajetan Errico, founder of the Missionaries of the Sacred Hearts, founded the Perpetual Cult to the Sacred Hearts in 1846 with a feast on the 4th Sunday after Pentecost.

[18] Various private revelations have indicated that this is what God desires at this time. Some also suggest that this day might be a feast in honor of the Sacred Heart of Jesus and of the Immaculate Heart of Mary together.

Chapter Seven

CONSECRATION TO THE TWO HEARTS

One thing is obvious from the past three hundred years of world maturation: God is leading us to see the Hearts of Jesus and Mary *together* in the final effort to destroy the reign of Satan.

Due to St. John Eudes, the feast of the Immaculate Heart of Mary was celebrated for the first time in 1648, followed by the Sacred Heart in 1672, just a year before the appearance of the Sacred Heart at Paray in God's "final effort."[19] (The *combined* "Feast of the Sacred Hearts" was instituted in 1846.)

Speaking on the centenary of the consecration of the world to the Sacred Heart by Leo XIII, on June 4, 1999, Pope John Paul II said:

"Following St. John Eudes, who taught us *to contemplate Jesus, the Heart of hearts,* **in the Heart of Mary, and to make them both known and loved,** *devotion to the Sacred Heart has developed in the world* particularly because of St. Margaret Mary at Paray le Monial."[20]

A chosen soul with special insights into the devotion to the Sacred Hearts of Jesus and Mary was given to know that among the "greatest graces," which Pope Leo XIII foresaw

---

[19] Both feasts were double of the lst class with an octave but were later diminished. The feast honoring both Sacred Hearts on one day (4th Sun. after Pentecost) was instituted in Italy in 1846 and was also celebrated with great solemnity.

[20] *L'Osservatore Romano*, July 21, 1999 (Eng. Ed.).

(from the consecration of the world to the Sacred Heart), *was the Divine intervention at Fatima "to establish in the world devotion to the Immaculate Heart of Mary,* and the devotion to the Flame of Love of both their Hearts."

"To contemplate Jesus, the Heart of hearts, in the Immaculate Heart of Mary, and to make Them Both known and loved," as the Pope said on June 4, 1999, **is the unfolding of God's "final effort" to wrest mankind from the reign of Satan.**

Consecration to the Immaculate Heart of Mary is now *required* by God "**so that many souls will be saved**" and that *through this Immaculate Heart will come the triumph of the Heart of Jesus.*

We can understand Fatima, and understand where we are in the "Fatima week," only if we see the Fatima message indeed as an unfolding of the message of Jesus from Paray le Monial where St. Margaret Mary was inspired to honor the Hearts of Jesus and Mary as ONE Heart—as have other saints, such as St. Jane de Chantal, St. Francis de Sales, St. John Eudes.

Not Equal but One Flame of Love

St. John Eudes was perhaps the first to speak of the "Sacred Heart of Mary." He was born in France in 1601, forty six years before St. Margaret Mary Alacoque. He had a major role in *the unfolding of God's plan for consecration to the Two Hearts.* He composed the Mass and office of the Immaculate Heart and the Mass and office of the Sacred Heart. And *he joined the Two Hearts.* He spoke of them as one.[21] (See inside front cover.)

Also in the beautiful prayer taught by God the Father to Mother Eugenia, we say: "*I come to You with Jesus and Mary to ask...*" And then after making petitions, we say: "*In union with Their Hearts,* I offer You sacrifices, etc."

---

[21] St. John Eudes is described by Charles Lebrun as "the author of the liturgical worship of the SACRED HEARTS." One of his greatest works is *Le Coeur Admirable de la tres sacrée Mere de Dieu.* For a summary, see the author's book *Her Glorious Title,* the first chapters of which quote this work of St. John Eudes extensively.

The words may give us pause. But the reality, when experienced, is transcendentally beautiful. It is the realization that the Hearts of Jesus and Mary are two flames which God has joined together into one great flame of love for Him and for men. And we, poor creatures, can plunge the little love we have into that great flame where it, too, becomes one with it.

When we grasp this, we no longer pause. We take the leap of love. We are no longer worried about speaking of the Sacred Hearts as one. We know this does not mean that the Two Hearts are equal. Indeed, one is human and the other Divine. It merely means that the flames of Their love are as one flame. And we, as humans, identifying ourselves with the human heart of Mary, enter into that Flame of Love to be truly one with the Heart of Our Savior.

The words of Our Lord to St. John Eudes seem to say it all: "I have given you this admirable Heart of My dear Mother to be one with yours, so that you might have a heart worthy of Mine."

This is not a matter of our choice, but of God's choice. This is not a matter of our planning as the way to become intimate with our Father God, but of His.

We deserve chastisement. God's final effort to save us is through *love.*

Now Two Hearts

That is why His final effort began with the revelation of the flaming Heart of Jesus and why it comes to a climax now in the revelation of the flaming Heart of Mary.

At Pellevoisin, in 1876, Our Lady made a new revelation of devotion to the Two Hearts, referring to the Scapular (the sign of consecration to Her Immaculate Heart) as "My livery and *that of My Son.*"

It is interesting to note that 1876 was the year Our Lady foretold the death of St. Catherine Labouré, to whom She had revealed the medal of the Two Hearts, and in that same year, She brought back from the brink of death another messenger of a new revelation of the Sacred Hearts: Estelle Faguette. One has the impression of a time-calibrated unfolding of God's final effort, the unfolding of the Sacred Hearts.

Referring to the message of Our Lord to St. Margaret Mary, Our Lady told Estelle: "*For a long time the treasures of My Son have been opened.*" (Indeed, for two hundred years!) Then, She invited Estelle to kiss the Scapular on which appeared the Sacred Heart, "complete and as usually represented according to the revelations of the Sacred Heart at Paray le Monial."[22] And kissing the Scapular on Our Lady's breast, Estelle was intensely aware of the Heart of Mary. *She felt one in the flame of Love of the Sacred Hearts.*

Now, more than another hundred years later, is the world ready for this? Can such a great effort of love win *our* hearts?

We Have Deserved Chastisement

We were told at Fatima, in 1917, that if we ignored the merciful gift and requests of God's Love, we would suffer the second world war (we were informed even of the time it would begin). We were told the world would be engulfed in the spread of militant atheism from Russia throughout the entire world "fostering further wars," that millions would be persecuted and martyred, and that the Pope would suffer.

We ignored the requests. We deserved it all. *We even merit the last prophecy not yet fulfilled: "Several entire nations will be annihilated."*

But, through the Immaculate Heart, a great promise has been made. It is a promise that God's final effort to wrest mankind from Satan's empire will NOW succeed! It was confirmed by a great miracle. That promise is: "*Finally My Immaculate Heart will triumph. Russia will be converted and an era of peace will be granted to mankind.*"

And, it is not too late—until we are in the Bastille *with no one to hear us.*

The Promise

At this moment, we should be speaking of exactly what needs to be done to obtain this great promise. But first let us gaze at the very wonder of it.

---

[22] See *Her Glorious Title*, by John Haffert, pg 98.

It will be the greatest epoch in the history of man. Some say it will resemble Heaven on earth. According to the recognized revelations of Luisa Picaretta, it will be a fulfillment of the prayer of two thousand years to the Father: "Thy will be done on earth *as it is in Heaven.*"

We saw a glimpse of it in the very first apparition at Fatima. In the very light of Her Heart, Our Lady revealed what the coming triumph will be.

Light streamed from Her Heart causing the children of Fatima to feel "*lost in God,*" and to cry out: "O Most Holy Trinity, I adore Thee! My God, My God, I love Thee in the Most Blessed Sacrament!"

In that light from Her Heart, the children understood and were overwhelmed by the Love of the Eucharistic Heart of Her Son. Blessed Francis, the nine-year-old visionary of Fatima, from that time had but one thought: *to console the hidden Jesus* TRULY present in our tabernacles, for Whom the angel of Fatima had asked prayers of reparation "*for the outrages, sacrileges and indifference by which He is offended.*"

The effect of that light from the Heart of Mary was a certain sign of the coming triumph of Grace in the world which, at the time of the revelations of the Sacred Heart, had been prophesied by St. Grignion de Montfort. He said that as Jesus came the first time through Mary, so he would bring about *His triumph* through Her.

As the Two Hearts were united at the word of an angel and united on Calvary, so They would be united in turning back the tidal wave of evil and bring the world into the new era of a peace—*a peace flowing from their combined Flame of Love.*

The first step to be taken is our act of consecration. "*As we near the third millennium,*" Pope John Paul II said in the message for the centenary of the collegial consecration to the Sacred Heart on June 4, 1999, "*the love of Christ impels us*' (2 Cor. 5:14) to make known and love the Savior Who shed His Blood for mankind. '*For their sake, I consecrate Myself, that they also may be consecrated in truth*' (John, 17:19)."[23]

Again, the Pope seems to confirm what we have been saying about the *unfolding* of God's final effort to save man from self destruction by consecration to His Merciful Love, manifested in the Sacred Heart of Jesus and the Immaculate Heart of Mary.

The Consecration

This consecration, as we have already said, means simply the choice away from the love of sin to the love of these Hearts which, for love of us, together on Calvary, overcame the punishment of original sin and opened the gates of Heaven.

Consecration is asked of the world, of nations, of dioceses, of families, and of individuals to these Two Hearts. We are commanded to renew these consecrations in some formal way at least once a year. It has been suggested that an appropriate day for this annual renewal would be on the feasts of their Hearts, or on the Sunday immediately thereafter.

In his consecration of the world to the Immaculate Heart of Mary, Pope John Paul II prayed:

"Before you, Mother of Christ, before your Immaculate Heart, I today, together with the whole Church, unite myself with our Redeemer in this consecration for the world and for people for whom *only His Divine Heart* has the power to obtain pardon and to secure reparation."

The consecration to the Immaculate Heart of Mary is related to consecration to the Sacred Heart in an ineffable manner. It can be grasped in Divine light, but cannot be grasped by mere reason. It can be explained only for the very same reason that God created us in the first place: Love.

Summary of the Requests of Fatima

By "consecration," we are set aside. We make a choice to belong to what is pure and holy. **And ultimately it is the personal consecration, the setting aside of *ourselves*, which will weigh down the scales of**

---

[23] *L'Osservatore Romano*, July 21, 1999 (Eng. Ed.).

Divine Justice, and prevent the annihilation of various nations.

For this personal response, one would like to insert here the entire text of at least three other books[24] adequately to explain the devotions Our Lady held out to us at Fatima as aids to be "set aside"—*the Scapular and the Rosary.*

But what was said in many hundreds of pages, we will try to say in a few paragraphs:

The first request of Our Lady of Fatima is sanctification of daily duty, and She offers especially two devotions (the Scapular and the Rosary) to help us. They make all the difference.

Just Offer What We Already Do!

Daily duty is simply keeping the commandments. Many people, even without religion, feel compelled, often under penalty of civil law, to keep them. But Our Lady asks us *to offer up the sacrifice this effort requires to obtain graces for those who do not keep them.*

After showing **a vision of hell, "where the souls of poor sinners go,"** She said: *"To save them, God wishes to establish in the world devotion to my Immaculate Heart. If what I say to you is done, many souls will be saved and there will be peace."*

Souls will be saved not just by consecration to the Immaculate Heart of Mary, which is facilitated and more completely fulfilled through the devotions of the Scapular and the Rosary, but especially by the special fruit of that consecration: **A joining with Our Lady *in making reparation* for the sins of the world.**

For this, Our Lady provides a special, very powerful practice, *which She asks us to perform only five times in our life.*

---

[24] *Sign of Her Heart*, book on the Scapular; *Sex and the Mysteries*, book on the Rosary; *Her Glorious Title*, book on the use of both in the ascent to holiness. (See inside back cover.)

CHAPTER EIGHT

COMMUNIONS OF REPARATION

That which is especially asked of us now, and which the bishops of the world are asked to promote in this post-consecration period, is *the "reparatory" devotion of the First Saturdays.*

For those who may not know this devotion, we will summarize it here. (Those who know all about it, or have read the author's book *Too Late?*, might just scan through to the next chapter.)

The details of the devotion were given to Sister Lucia while she was a postulant in the convent of the Dorothean Sisters in Pontevedra, Spain, on December 10, 1925, although it had been previously announced to her at Fatima eight years before.

Our Lady appeared in Lucia's tiny room (only about three feet between the little bed and the wall) with the Child Jesus at Her side. Her Heart shone through, pierced by many thorns. The Holy Child, elevated so that Lucia could look into His eyes at the same time that she looked into the eyes of His Mother, was the first to speak:

"Have compassion on the Heart of your most holy Mother, covered with thorns with which ungrateful men pierce it at every moment, and there is no one to make an act of reparation to remove them!"

Loving Intimacy

The space in the little room was so narrow that Our Lady *was resting Her hand on Lucia's shoulder*, making this one of the most intimate of all recorded apparitions. Lucia was deeply saddened by the words of the Holy Child as He referred to Our Lady's suffering heart as *the heart of YOUR Mother!* (Oh, how intimately the thorns and love of Her Heart make us one with Jesus!)

"Look, my daughter," Our Lady now said, *"at my heart surrounded with thorns with which ungrateful men pierce it at every moment by their blasphemies and ingratitude... You at least try to console me."*

In this intimate apparition, Our Lord said: "Behold the heart of your Most Holy Mother covered with thorns..." Our Lady asked for Communions of Reparation on five First Saturdays.

Our Lady then made the great promise, already mentioned above, to all who would fulfill the following conditions:

"On the first Saturday of five consecutive months—confess, receive Holy Communion, recite five decades of the Rosary, and keep me company for fifteen minutes while meditating on the mysteries of the Rosary, with the intention of making reparation to me."

Jesus Comes Back

Lucia told the Prioress about the request of Our Lady and of the Holy Child for this First Saturday devotion. The superior replied that there was nothing she could do about it. And without the support of the superior, what could Lucia do? She was filled with concern.

On February 26, 1926, while she was transferring waste from a cesspool to a street sewer, a little boy, who seemed to be passing by, paused at the gate.

He seemed sad and lonely. "Don't you have anyone to play with?" she asked. The boy did not reply. Something about him, and his sadness, caused Lucia to ask if he knew the Hail Mary. He remained silent, sad. She had her duties to fulfill. Was there any way she could console him?

"Why don't you go around the corner to the Church of St. Mary Major and ask Our Lady to give you the Child Jesus to keep you company?"

At that, the little boy was transformed. It was Jesus, just as she had seen him six weeks before with Our Lady in her little room.

Although transformed, He was still sad as He asked: "What is being done to promote the devotion to the Immaculate Heart of My Mother in the world?"

Pausing in astonishment from her lowly work, and struck by the same sadness, Lucia answered: "I told the Mother Superior and she said there was nothing she could do."

"*Of herself, no,*" Jesus replied, "*but with My Grace, she can do it all.*"

What Is Being Done?

To set an example to the world, Pope John Paul II has personally led the First Saturday Rosary month after month, year in and year out, during the later years of his Pontificate.

But it seems that this devotion depends on each of us.

When the Holy Child said that even the Dorothean Prioress could, with His grace, do all that was needed to promote this devotion, was He not speaking to each of us? With His grace, can we not all become successful apostles in proclaiming Our Lady's great promise, and the desire of the Sacred Hearts for this simple devotion?

Much depends upon it.

When Our Lady first announced this devotion, She had made a series of prophecies ending in the words: "*Several entire nations will be annihilated.*" Then, She said that She would come to ask for this devotion, these First Saturday Communions of Reparation, "*TO PREVENT THIS.*"

From the time Our Lady said this at Fatima, on July 13, 1917, little Jacinta who had not been old enough to make her first Communion, often said: "I am so grieved not to be able to receive Communion in reparation for the sins committed against the Immaculate Heart of Mary!"

But *why is Holy Communion* the object of reparation? Why on First Saturdays, and why accompanied by the Rosary, fifteen minutes of meditation, and confession even if we are not in mortal sin?

What Most Offends Their Sacred Hearts

Anything which offends the Heart of Jesus offends the Heart of His Mother. The greatest offenses are those directly against Our Lord Himself in the Sacrament of His Love.

Our Lady said at Pellevoisin: "What most offends my Immaculate Heart are *careless Communions.*"

Today, how many Communions are not only careless but even sacrilegious!

Our Lord had asked for Communions of Reparation to His Sacred Heart on nine First Fridays. And now He reminds us of the same thorns piercing the Heart of His

Mother. He asks for Communions of Reparation to HER Immaculate Heart. We are asked to prepare ourselves for that Communion by confession, fifteen minutes of meditation, and by praying the Rosary.

What Most Consoles Their Sacred Hearts

More and more generous souls are saying:

"Dear Lord, You ask so little on the First Fridays to console Your Heart; You ask so little on First Saturdays to console *our* Mother's Heart.

"We will give Your Sacred Hearts not just those few hours, but the entire night! We will begin on First Friday evening, in honor of Your Sacred Heart, and keep You company in the Sacrament of Your Love to the morning of First Saturday, in honor of the Immaculate Heart of Mary!"

These are known as the Vigils of the Two Hearts.

Thousands of generous souls throughout the world are now making this response. Some feel it is this which will tip the balance of God's Justice.

Our Lord said to Lucia in March, 1939:

"Ask, ask again insistently for the promulgation of the Communion of Reparation in honor of the Immaculate Heart of Mary on the First Saturdays. The time is coming when the rigor of My Justice will punish the crimes of diverse nations. Some of them will be annihilated. At last the severity of My Justice will fall severely on those who want to destroy My Reign in souls." (*Documentos*, pg. 465).

Why Five?

St. Pius X indulgenced the devotion for twelve First Saturdays. Granting still further indulgences, Pope Benedict XV made it eight. Our Lady, extending the conditions, made it five. Why?

One might suppose first of all that Our Lady wanted to ask of us as little as necessary to change us and to change the world. But Sister Lucia explains further:

"While in the chapel with Our Lord part of the night between the 29th and 30th of May, 1930, while speaking to Our Good Lord about this question, I felt myself being more possessed by the Divine Presence and the following was made known to me:

"Jesus said: 'My daughter, the reason is simple. There are five ways by which people offend and blaspheme against the Immaculate Heart of Mary:

1) Blasphemies against Her Immaculate Conception;

2) Blasphemies against Her Virginity;

3) Blasphemies against Her Divine Maternity, refusing at the same time to accept Her as the Mother of all mankind;

4) Those who try publicly to implant in the hearts of children indifference, contempt, and even hatred against this Immaculate Mother;

5) Those who insult Her directly in Her sacred images.

"'Here, My daughter, are the reasons why the Immaculate Heart of Mary compelled Me to ask for this little act of reparation and, due to it, to move My Mercy to forgive those souls who had the misfortune of offending Her. As for you, try unceasingly with all your prayers and sacrifices to move Me to Mercy toward those poor souls.'"

Must It Be On Saturday?

Saturday is "Our Lady's Day" because on the Saturday after Good Friday, Our Lady's passion continued. She suffered not only the aftermath of Calvary but the knowledge that Her Jesus was dead. She longed to be with Him in the tomb. At the same time, She suffered because the apostles were scattered. She worried especially about Judas and Peter. She was now the Mother of the Church.

Therefore, it is ideal to fulfill all four conditions of the First Saturday on the day itself, all with the intention of making reparation—of helping to remove the thorns encircling Her maternal Heart.

However Our Lord told Lucia that, for a good reason, His priests may change the day as, for example, when no priest is available on the Saturday but only on the next day, a Sunday.

Also, it has become common practice *for the all-night vigils* to choose *the Saturday after First Friday* on the rare occasions when a Saturday may fall on the first day of the month.

Confession Even If Not In Mortal Sin

One of the essential conditions of the First Saturday devotion is confession.

It may be within eight days provided the recipient of First Saturday Communion is in the state of Grace. But again, it is advisable to go to confession *on the First Saturday (or prior to the First Friday Communion) if possible.*

A great advantage of the night vigil is that one fulfills the requests of the Sacred Heart for First Friday, and of the Immaculate Heart for First Saturday, at the same time. And during the night, there is ample time for confession, for the fifteen minute meditation, for the Rosary, and above all, for the making of a truly worthy Communion of Reparation. Fittingly, the vigils have come to be known as "The Night of Love." (For further information on the vigils, see book of this same name, *The Night Of Love*, see inside back cover.)

"Keep Me Company"

One of the wonders of the First Saturdays is the invitation of Our Lady to "*keep me company* for fifteen minutes, while meditating on the mysteries of the Rosary."

At the moment of the epiphany of Jesus in the temple, there was an epiphany of Our Lady's Heart. While seeing the Savior of the world, the prophet Simeon saw Our Lady's Heart. "*Your own Heart a sword will pierce,*" the holy man exclaimed, "*that out of many hearts thoughts might be revealed.*"

This prophecy is fulfilled on the First Saturday as we keep Mary company, as we share in the mysteries of Her Heart and of the Heart of Jesus.

It is not so much that we keep Our Lady company as that She keeps company with us!

The great Marian apostle of Poland, Anatol Kaszczuk, exclaimed: "Oh, how I look forward to the First Saturdays, when Our Lady shares with us the mysteries of Her Heart!"

It is a blessed experience.

"These Souls Will Be Beloved"

In the apparition of June 13, 1917, Our Lady told the children of Fatima: "Jesus wishes to use you to make Me known and loved. *He wishes to establish in the world devotion to My Immaculate Heart.* To those who embrace it, I promise salvation, and these souls will be beloved by God, like flowers placed by Me to adorn His Throne."

The beatification of the two younger children of Fatima, Francis and Jacinta, was approved by Pope John Paul II in June, 1999. The message of reparation to the Immaculate Heart of Mary which made them saints was at the heart of the entire Fatima message.

When Our Lady promised, in 1917, to come "soon" to take Francis and Jacinta to Heaven, Lucia asked sadly, "Must I stay here alone?"

Our Lady answered: "No, My daughter, *I will never forsake you. My Immaculate Heart will be your consolation, and the way that will lead you to God.*"

Do we wish to be souls beloved of God? Do we wish to be like flowers placed by Our Lady Herself to adorn His Throne? Do we wish never to be alone, always having Her Immaculate Heart as our consolation, and the way that will lead us to God?

Special Blessings

These are the blessings of this devotion!

What is more, when enough persons are fulfilling the basic requests of Our Lady by means of the Scapular, Rosary, and Morning Offering, and by completing the Five First Saturdays, we will see more wonders in the world, just as we saw the sudden downfall of the Soviet Union.

Annihilation of nations may be prevented.

The reign of the Sacred Hearts has been promised at Fatima. That promise has been confirmed by Our Lady of All Nations. The love of the Hearts of Jesus and Mary will bring peace to the nations of the world.

It is now up to the laity to make the first move.

CHAPTER NINE

THAT FINAL LESSON: IMPORTANCE OF THE LAITY

Jesus Himself, as we have repeated, compared the delay in reaction to the requests of His Sacred Heart to the delay in responding to those of his Mother's Immaculate Heart. All became "transparent and comprehensible" to the Holy Father "in the light of history and the signs of the times."

What was the final lesson of the history of response to the requests of the Sacred Heart?

It was the intervention of lay persons.

And this lesson is not merely historical.

Appearing in our time as Our Lady of All Nations, Queen of the World, Our Lady foretold Her victory and said: "The clergy are too few...*mobilize the laity.*"

At the same time, God gave the world a continuing miracle in the person of Marthe Robin, who lived thirty years solely on the Eucharist, and who said: "*The laity will renew the Church.*"

Great Hope

It is one of the greatest lessons and messages of our time that God inspired the laity, after more than two hundred years of widespread suffering in the wake of the refusal to obey the Sacred Heart, to do two things: to ask the Archbishop to intervene and offer to help.

Our one great hope is that the laity will do the same now.

In his apostolic letter for the new millennium, the Pope saw *three main signs of hope in the Church*: deeper commitment to the cause of Christian unity, and "*greater attention to the voice of the Holy Spirit, through acceptance of charisms and promotion of the laity.*"[25]

Since the second Vatican Council, there has been a virtual explosion of lay involvement in the life of the Church. In a moment, we will cite a few in the hope that others may be inspired. But first, let us emphasize that this call is not just from Our Lady of All Nations, or from mystics like Marthe Robin, or from the example of the laymen who broke the two hundred year lack of response to the requests of the Sacred Heart.

It is the call of the Holy Spirit. It is the call of the Church.

Modern Conditions Demand It

In the very opening statement of its Decree on the Apostolate of the Laity, the Council said: "Modern conditions demand that the lay apostolate be thoroughly broadened and intensified."

The Council said that "an indication of this manifold and pressing need is *the unmistakable work of the Holy Spirit in making the Laity today more conscious of their own responsibility.*"

The Holy Spirit, Who inspired Pope John XXIII to convene the second Vatican Council (as the Pope himself declared), was providing for this present time when the role of the laity will be of supreme importance. The Council has reminded EVERY Catholic that it is not just up to the clergy, but to each and every one of us as "sharers in the priestly, prophetic, and royal office of Christ" (i. 2).

In the Light of Fatima

The message of Fatima is like a flood of light over this era of the second Vatican Council. Our Lady stooped down to children, and called them to join Her in saving the world —in bringing about the triumph of the Church, for that is

---

[25] *Tertio Millennio Adveniente*, par. 46.

what is meant in Her promise of the triumph of Her Immaculate Heart.

She told them to pray the Rosary. She told them to think of Her Immaculate Heart—the ultimate symbol of purity—and to be united to that Heart. She held the Scapular out of the sky as She performed a "great miracle so that all may believe."

As a loving Mother, She reduces it all down to the level of little children—seven, nine, and ten years of age, two of whom have already been declared to be in Heaven. We have thought of the Fatima message in the terms of bringing an end to world communism and preventing atomic war. It is time we began thinking of it in terms of *Christifideles Laici,* issued December 30, 1988, by Pope John Paul II (English translation published by the Daughters of St. Paul), in which the Holy Father sees a revitalized, responsible laity as *the greatest need of our time.*

His Holiness applies to lay Catholics the words of Our Lord: "Why do you stand here idle all the day?... You, too, go into My Vineyard." (Mt 20:3-4). The entire last part of the Pope's message calls for a continual process of development of holiness in the laity, and of *acceptance of its responsibility.*

I have written an entire book on this subject titled *You, Too!.* I do not wish to belabor it here other than to say that as the Holy Father sees the recognition of charisms, and the response of the laity, as two of the three main signs of hope in the Church, that hope is gone if we ignore the charisms and if the laity do NOT respond. The time for saying it is up to the Pope, it is up to the bishops, it is up to the priests, is *over.*

It is up to us. God will hold us responsible.

The consequences of our failure to respond, of which we shall speak in a moment, are terrible almost beyond imagining.

Chapter Ten

LAST EFFORT

On such an important subject it may seem arrogant for an author to intrude personal opinions or views. But I feel I should do so because of my rather unique role in the unfolding intervention of God at Fatima.

In my own experience, which began in 1933 and spanned sixty-seven years, the Fatima message seemed essentially *for the present moment.* I seemed blind, for example, to the words of Our Lord that the response of one Pope after the other would be like that of three succeeding kings of France. And it came as a total surprise when Sister Lucia said, on the eve of the new millennium, that "The Fatima week *has just begun."*

The circumstances in which Sister Lucia made this statement signaled its importance. It was carefully prepared. She was fluent in Spanish, in which she had been speaking to the Cardinal. But she turned to an interpreter and said that she wished to make *this* statement in her own language (Portuguese).

That was to me a sign that Our Lord or Our Lady (her usual sources) had given her this statement. And it may be her final word, after more than eighty years of messages from God, to the atomic age.

My Reasons

My own involvement in the message began with a vision to a holy Carmelite brother, now long since gone, of which I wrote in one of my earliest books *The Brother and I.* The basic message of Fatima was revealed to him in 1933, at a time when neither he nor I had heard of Fatima. He was told that God would save the world by means of a simple formula: To live the morning offering (sanctification of daily duty) with the aid of the Scapular and the Rosary. And I was to help make it known to the world.

Thirteen years later, in a more than three hour interview with Sister Lucia, I was awed by her confirmation.

I was more than awed. It seemed unbelievable. I had thought the main thrust of the message of Fatima was the Rosary. Had I influenced her because of the Brother's vision? I went to the Bishop of Fatima (who had sent me to Sister Lucia in the first place) for direction.

Almost without hesitation, the bishop said that this was indeed the basic message of Fatima. He added: "You may promulgate this *as coming from me.*"

The Other Days?

A "march of pledges" began under the auspices of the bishop. It became popularly known as the Blue Army, and was ultimately recognized by the Church as the World Apostolate of Fatima. The number of pledges, in over a hundred countries, exceeded twenty five million.

But after the change in Russia, with the exception of places still under threat, like South Korea, the apostolate dwindled. Now, at the time when God requires the First Saturday Communions of Reparation, the apostolate's network of communications had become crippled (as described in my book *The Day I Didn't Die*, published in 1998).

But did not the statement that Fatima has just begun mean *that the need to make the message heard is undiminished?*

What will day four be? And how close is it?

Unfolding

It has for me been a constant source of surprise and wonder that everything in the apostolate has seemed to take so much longer than expected. I would anticipate something "tomorrow" and it would happen months or years later.

Is it not a cause for wonder that the light of devotion to the Hearts of Jesus and Mary was first seen by some individual saints and mystics (like St. Gertrude) some *thousand years after the gospels were written?*

It is also striking that it was St. John the Evangelist who told St. Gertrude that the reason he had not written of the Sacred Heart in his gospel was because he was writing for the Church "in its infancy." And, **almost four hundred years** later, *it was on the feast of St. John the Evangelist, December 27, 1673, that St. Margaret Mary Alacoque had the first of the apparitions which have opened the entire Church to this devotion.*

Last Effort of His Love

"Before the Blessed Sacrament, I was so overwhelmed by this Divine Presence as to forget myself and the place where I was," the saint tells us, adding: "He (Our Lord) allowed me to recline for a long time on His Divine Breast, where He disclosed to me the marvels of His love and the unutterable secrets of His Sacred Heart, which He had always concealed from me."

Now was finally the time when Jesus was *going to reveal his Heart*, through this hidden saint, to *us.* He said:

"My Divine Heart is passionately inflamed *with love for men* that, not being able any longer to contain within Itself the flames of It's ardent charity, It must need spread them abroad through your means, and manifest Itself to men that they may be enriched with It's precious treasures."

St. Margaret Mary relates that in his next appearance to her, Jesus said: ***"This devotion was the last effort of His love that He would grant to men in the last centuries of the world in order to withdraw them from the empire of Satan which He desired to destroy...."***[26]

---

[26] *Vie et Oeuvres*, vol. 2, 4th letter to P. Croisete, 1690, pgs. 571-73. Cf: *Devotion to the Sacred Heart*, by Louis Verheylezoon, S.J., Sands & Co., 1955, xiv.

CHAPTER ELEVEN

SERIOUS CONSEQUENCES

While filled with questioning wonder at the slow unfolding of the manifestation of God's Love in the Hearts of Jesus and Mary, and of His invitation for us to place our own hearts into Their Flame of Love, are we not at the same time left in amazement at the consequences of failure to respond?

We are shocked at the sad sight of Louis XVI beheaded in the Place de la Concorde, leaving behind in the Bastille his final desperate vow to respond when it was too late. But even all the wars of the last two hundred years could hardly enable us even to grasp the magnitude of the consequences of that failure.

This book is based on the startling message given by Sister Lucia in 1993, and so far we have revealed only part of it —the part about the Fatima week and that the triumph is an "ongoing process."

But she also said that ALL THE WARS SINCE 1918 COULD HAVE BEEN PREVENTED.

How Could It Be?

Anatol Kaszczuk, the great Marian apostle of Poland, tells of his shock at the suffering and death in Warsaw during the German invasion. When over 200,000, had died he asked a priest in the confessional how God could permit such "global" atrocities. To his surprise, the priest said:

"To know the answer you must know the message of Fatima."

That was back in 1940 when most of the world had not heard anything about Fatima. The "great sign" given by God in 1938, although seen by millions, had been ignored.

The Great Sign

Do we know of any other times in History that God has gone to such great lengths to get our attention, to save us from ourselves?

It was in 1917 that Our Lady, after prophesying the second world war which would be "worse than the first," said that God would give a sign so that people would be warned. She said:

"When you will see the night illumined by an unknown light you will know that it is the great sign that God is about to punish the world."

GREAT SIGN indeed! On the night of January 25, 1938, it seemed that half the world was on fire. A seminarian in Vienna recalls that it seemed the city and the country about was all in flames. When one of the seminary professors said it was probably *the great sign of Fatima*, and that a war was about to begin, no one asked: What *does the Fatima message say we must DO to prevent it?*

Consequences

It does not sum it up simply to say that many MILLIONS died. One would need to know HOW those millions died, and how much those who survived suffered—sometimes for the rest of their lives. And it would be necessary to reduce those millions to just one or two individuals, perhaps to one man starved to death in a prison like St. Maximilian Kolbe. Or would it be a woman with children walking out of the ruins of Nagasaki with all their skin burned off, slowly dying?

Perhaps we are tired of seeing war films and war documentaries. We are tired of hearing of the horrors. We no longer like to look at the sea of white crosses in the military cemeteries scattered all over Europe and in the Pacific. The horror was global and it ended in the greatest single horror of all: Hiroshima and Nagasaki.

And it all—*all* could have been avoided. Our Lady had said:

"If my requests are heard..." And in the third day, She is still saying: "If my requests are heard...an era of peace will be granted to mankind."

Magnitude Difficult to Grasp

As I brought out in my book *Too Late?*, we do not have to go back to the horrors of the second world war, which engulfed most of the world. Consider just the scale of the killings in Rwanda and the Balkans, in both of which countries Our Lady had appeared ten years before the killings to remind the people of Her message.

In ratio to the population of the United States, in *each* of those countries the number killed would equal about *twenty five MILLION*.

It was at the very time Our Lady was reported to be giving messages in Rwanda and in the Balkans that the Bishop of Akita in Japan announced, on March 27, 1982, that Our Lady had come **with a similar reminder for the entire world**:

*"Many people in this world afflict the Lord. If they do not repent and better themselves, the Father will inflict a terrible punishment **on all humanity**."*

As in Rwanda, we are told specifically what the punishment will be. Instead of a river of blood it will be fire:

"It will be a punishment worse than the deluge, such as one will never have seen before. Fire will fall from the sky and will wipe out a great part of humanity... The survivors will find themselves so desolate that they will envy the dead."

"Will Envy the Dead"

If we ignore this message, the predicted punishment will now affect ALL humanity. And we have already had half a century to respond because, in the very words of the Bishop of Akita: "It is the message of Fatima."

But we have largely ignored the part of the message of Fatima which states that the alternative to our response will be the annihilation of entire nations. Perhaps the reason it is ignored is precisely because it is so terrible, so unthinkable.

To many, the most terrible part of the prophecy of Akita seems to be in those words: *"The survivors will find themselves so desolate that they will envy the dead."*

Indeed, this prophecy is so terrible that, even after nine years of inquiries, the local Bishop hesitated to publish it. He went to Rome for advice. *Cardinal Ratzinger, custodian of the third secret of Fatima, reassured him that what Our Lady said at Akita was substantially the same as what She revealed in the secret of Fatima.*

This was told to me personally by the bishop. Later, Cardinal Ratzinger confirmed it in an interview with the Honorable Howard Dee when the latter was leaving Rome after serving as the Philippine Ambassador to the Holy See. It was published in Dee's important book *Mankind's Final Destiny.*

We people of the third millennium, who have ignored the message of Fatima, are warned that if the requests of Our Lady continue to be ignored, "several entire nations will be annihilated." It will be by fire. And it will affect *all humanity.*

Will it be too late for us? Will we continue to ignore the alternative of fire engulfing the earth and wiping out "a great part of humanity?"

Yet, *we know what we can do* to prevent it!

Indeed, we do not tire of recalling that Our Lady said at Akita that SO FAR, *She **has** been able to prevent it* because of the response of a few! And she said:

*"Pray very much the prayers of the Rosary. I alone **am able still to save you from the calamities which approach.** Those who place their confidence in me will be saved."*

Chapter Twelve

A MESSAGE OF LOVE

When we think of all the suffering that befell France during the 200 years following the refusal of the King of France to fulfill the simple requests in return for which Jesus promised "*My protection*" and "*Victory over all your enemies,*" we might tend to think that *it was all a "punishment"* of God for the failure to respond.

The truth is quite, quite different.

The sufferings could have been prevented. Devotion to the Sacred Heart *could have turned that nation, then very Catholic, from the degeneration* which climaxed in the French revolution. The world could have avoided two hundred years of wars and bitter persecution of religion culminating in the atheist revolution in Russia, which was the evil spawn of the French revolt.

Are we now surprised when Sister Lucia said, in the historic 1993 interview, that *all the wars since 1917 could have been prevented* if we had responded to Our Lord's desire "To place devotion to the Immaculate Heart of My Mother alongside devotion to My Own Sacred Heart?"

Our sins have brought all this suffering into the world. The Hearts of Jesus and Mary are shown to us now *to draw us from sin.* Our acts of consecration are just that: *a renunciation of what would displease Their Hearts.*

And there is a special reason why devotion to the Immaculate Heart of Mary is now required by God to draw men from the reign of Satan. *This devotion to the Immaculate Heart of Mary is now **necessary.***

The world has so degenerated since rejection of the appeal of the Sacred Heart in 1673 that now we are told at Fatima: "Only She (the Immaculate Heart) can help you."

"Only She Can Help You"

Again the meaning of these words is quite different from what it first appears. The meaning is that *we have gone so far from God*, so far from the offered treasures of the Sacred Heart of Jesus, that *we seem no longer capable of turning away from our sins* and **God sends "the Mother" to help us.**

It is as though the saving treasures are on a table, and we are starving on the floor too weak to reach them.

The greatest of those saving treasures is the Eucharist. We can reach up through the Sacrament of reconciliation *but not enough of us seem to have the light and strength to do so.*

Our Lady reaches down the cords of Her Scapular and the chain of Her Rosary to lift us up. At the same time, She makes great promises for individuals and for the world to induce us.

In a word, although we deserve God's chastisement, as Blessed Jacinta of Fatima explained: *In His Mercy, He has entrusted the peace of the world to Her.* And in fulfillment of that mission, She comes with simple requests which even children can fulfill. Little things! Great rewards!

History Cries Out to Us

At our Lay Saints Retreat in July 1999, we heard a talk by a teacher of history (Sister Margaret Mary, of the Sisters of the Holy Trinity), who explained with great earnestness the need to heed the requests of the Hearts of Jesus and Mary. She concluded by saying that in all her study of history she saw no reference to such events as Paray le Monial and Fatima but, *in these events of the Two Hearts, all this history is explained.*

That is a truth at once revealing and frightening

It reveals God's intervention in the affairs of nations. It also reveals an almost universal rejection of this Divine intervention—this final effort of His constant Love to deliver us from "degeneration, disaster, and war."[27]

In His great Love, after revealing His flaming Heart when we were first getting into great danger, He now sends "the Mother" to promise us, if we will but turn to Him, that we shall have a triumph of love, an "era of peace for mankind."

He points to the Heart of His Mother in the Fatima intervention and says: "Behold the Heart of *your* Mother..." And She says: "Behold the Heart of your Saviour. *The treasures of His Heart have long been open and I come to help you obtain them.*"[28]

Why Are These Treasures Rejected?

St. Margaret Mary says Jesus revealed His Heart that men "might be enriched with the abundance and profusion of *those Divine treasures of which this Heart is the source...* He revealed to me the unspeakable marvels of His pure love, and the excess of love He had conceived for

---

[27] Words taught by Our Lady of all Nations in the prayer for today's world.

[28] The reader may recall that these are almost the very words Our Lady used at Pellevoisin.

men... He assured me that the pleasure He takes *in being loved, known, and honored by His creatures is so great that He promises that no one dedicated and consecrated to Him will ever perish.*"

In another place, the Saint adds: "His eager desire of imparting graces of sanctification and salvation to well-disposed hearts causes Him to wish to be known, adored, and glorified by His creatures."

Father Verheylezoon remarks: "In this desire of Our Lord, there is no shadow of egoism. He wishes to be loved *to induce us to love GOD His Father* and to pour upon the world the riches of His Love."

God sent His only Son into the world *to reveal that He is Love.* He said the night before His Heart was pierced on a cross: "When you see Me, you see the Father." He shows us a Heart flaming with Love *to remind us prodigal children* that there is nothing that Love will not forgive, and that His Love longs to save us from degeneration, disaster, and the atomic war which will wipe out much of humanity.

What Hope?

The specialty of the history teacher quoted above was the history of the 20th century. Immersion in this history for some forty years must have caused constant wonder that there was never a mention by the writers of history books of the intervention of God at Paray le Monial, which so affected the history of France, or at Fatima, which has so affected the entire world.

There was *no mention* in history of the two events which explain it.

What hope do we have of focusing attention on these interventions of God when they are so universally ignored and, when not ignored, rejected?

Despite the great miracle of Oct. 13, 1917, despite the great sign of 1938, and despite the sign of Russia's change in the wake of the collegial consecration of 1984, why do we continue to ignore the loving requests of the Hearts of Jesus and Mary?

One of the reasons is that too few of the laity realize that *they must be involved.*

CHAPTER THIRTEEN

FINAL APPEAL

The requests of the Sacred Heart from 1673 to 1689 were the beginning of the "final appeal" of God's Love. Let us read again the actual words of St. Margaret Mary describing that "final appeal" of our loving Savior as He held forth His Heart flaming with love:

"A final effort of His Love to favor human beings in the last centuries of the world and to withdraw them from the empire of Satan, which He intends to destroy and to replace with the reign of His Love."

Perhaps only now, after more than three hundred years, we can focus in on the words "*in the last centuries of the world.*"

This final effort was not to be limited by the whims of French kings. It was not to be limited by the refusal of a degenerating world to recognize in war after war, and persecution upon persecution, that it needed God's Love —that it HAD to respond or self-destruct.

This is finally what we have been told at Fatima.

Now we are shown the thorn encircled Heart of the Mother and told that the alternative is not a king on a guillotine. The alternative is that "several entire nations will be annihilated."

Pope John Paul II Chosen

The importance of this message is emphasized by the fact that God chose the Pope, the successor of St. Peter, to make it known to the world.

In the 17th century, Jesus revealed His final appeal to a cloistered nun.

How would she speak to the world? Did it not almost seem that Our Lord had made a mistake? But, he assured her:

"*I have chosen you for the accomplishment of this great design.*" When she asked how, He sent to her St. Claude de la Colombiere.

In "the Fatima week," after narrowly escaping death on May 13, 1981, **Pope John Paul II saw himself as chosen:** "*Perhaps this is why the Pope was called from a faraway country, perhaps this is why it was necessary for the assassination attempt to be made in St. Peter's Square precisely on May 13, 1981, the anniversary of the first apparition of Fatima...so that the voice of God...could more easily be heard and understood.*"

The Holy Father speaks with Sister Lucia at Fatima in 1982. His Holiness had come to thank Our Lady for his recovery from attempted assassination the previous May 13.

The Holy Father seems to be saying here that the accomplishment of the message of Fatima was *a reason for him to be called to the papacy.*

We have already seen to what lengths the Holy Father went in calling the attention of the entire world to the Fatima events. In October 1997, he spontaneously wrote a letter published in *L'Osservatore Romano* stating that Fatima was a great sign of our times not so much because of the miracle but because it indicates the specific response needed to save mankind from self-destruction.

That Urgent Message of the Pope

It is somewhat frightening that we live in a time when the Pope speaks and the world does not listen.

But if the world would not respect a miracle performed at a predicted time and place "so that all may believe," how can we expect the world to respect the voice of the Pope?

The October 13, 1997 message of the Pope concerning Fatima should be shaking the world and, if not the world, *at least the Church.*

The "Pope of Fatima," as John Paul II could be called, said (in *Tertio Millennio Adveniente*) there was another special reason he felt called to be Pope at this time: *To lead the world into the new millennium "in the hope of the definitive coming of the Kingdom."* And, he said that "As we approach the millennium, it seems that the words of Our Lady of Fatima are nearing their fulfillment."

Is this not the ultimate promise of the "final effort" of Divine Love "to withdraw men from the empire of Satan, which He intends to destroy and replace with the reign of His Love?"

More than three centuries have passed since those words were spoken at Paray. Soon we will have counted another century since the final effort of Divine Love was reinforced at Fatima with the revelation of the Immaculate Heart of Mary.

If we now join the words of the Immaculate Heart of His Mother to the words of Jesus concerning His Heart, the appeal of Love should finally compel us. Indeed the Pope said that the message of Fatima "compels the Church."

His Own Words

Every word spoken in reference to His Sacred Heart could be spoken of the Immaculate Heart of His Mother, which is one Flame of Love with His.

To better understand the revelation of the Immaculate Heart at Fatima, let us quote the words of the Sacred Heart to St. Margaret Mary, substituting "*Our* Sacred Hearts" for "*My* Divine Heart." In doing so, we find several important answers:

Q. Why No Longer be Contained?

A.: "Our Sacred Hearts are so passionately inflamed with love for men, and for you in particular, that *not being able any longer to contain the flames of Their ardent charity*, they must spread them abroad through your means."

Q. Why?

A. "That men may be enriched by Their salutary graces necessary to *hold them back from the abyss of ruin.*"

Q. How?

A. "*Offer your heart to Ours.*" (St. Margaret Mary suggested that we imagine taking our hearts into our hands and offering them to be engulfed in Their Flame of Love.)

Q. Why make reparation?

A. Both Hearts have been shown to us (at Paray and Fatima) *surrounded by thorns..."signifying the pricks in Them caused by your sins... Our Hearts have received nothing but ingratitude and contempt. This is more grievous to Us than all endured on Calvary. If they would only give Us some return of love, we should not reckon all that we have done for them, and we would do yet more if possible. But, they show only coldness and contempt for all Our endeavors to do them good. You, at least, can give Me the happiness of making up for their ingratitude.*"

How to make reparation? "*You are to receive Holy Communion on the First Friday (and Saturday) of each month.*"

Two Other Requests

In addition to the once a month Communion of Reparation, the Sacred Heart asked two things from the

Church in general: Consecration to His Heart, and a feast-day in honor of His Heart on the first Friday after the feast of Corpus Christi. The Church responded with the consecration and the feast.

For the Immaculate Heart of His Mother, at Fatima, He asked the same. The Church responded, placing the feast of the Immaculate Heart on the next day after the Feast of the Sacred Heart, and in 1996, made it an obligatory memorial. And the consecration was made by the Pope in union with all the bishops of the world.

The Final Vision

There were also two personal requests of the Sacred Heart: First He asked St. Margaret Mary to receive Communion as often as possible; Second, on the vigil of Friday: "You are to rise between eleven and twelve o'clock and remain with Me upon your knees for an hour...to appease the anger of My Eternal Father and to ask of Him pardon for sinners."

It was while making this very devotion in the chapel of Dorothean convent in Spain that Sister Lucia had *the final, and perhaps most meaningful of all the apparitions of Fatima.*

Jesus appeared hanging on the cross. Above Him were images of God the Father and the Holy Spirit.

From His Head and His Heart, Blood flowed down to a Host suspended above a chalice while, from His left Hand, there flowed down over the altar a stream (as of water) with the words "Graces and Mercy."

Beneath the right arm of the cross stood Our Lady, Her Immaculate Heart pierced with thorns.

A Book Could Not Contain It

A book many times larger than this would not have enough pages to explore all the mystery of this vision: The Trinity; Awareness that *GOD was on the cross;* Awareness that through this sacrifice, renewed in the Mass, GOD is with us in the Eucharist; Awareness that as the Blood flowed from the pierced Heart of Jesus, multiple thorns pierced the heart of His Mother.

We would like to make just one observation of a meaning not readily apparent: the meaning of Blood flowing ONLY from the Head and Heart of Jesus.

Obviously, this is a symbolic vision because He is alive on the cross, even though His Heart is pierced and Blood is flowing *only from His Head and His Heart.*

Blood actually flowed from Wounds all over His Body, pooling at His Feet. So why does this historic vision show Blood flowing only from Head and Heart?

My God, My God!

A *person* is defined as a being of intellect and will. And the flow of Blood from the Head and Heart of Jesus is seen as a reminder that on this cross is a DIVINE PERSON— One with God the Father and the Holy Spirit, Who are represented above Him on the cross by a Paternal Figure and a Dove.

Here are represented the presence of the other two Divine Persons of the Trinity as the Blood of Our Lord flows from His Head and His Heart, symbolizing His Person, One with the Person of the Father and the Holy Spirit as He redeems mankind.

This final vision of Fatima astoundingly carries us back to the very first appearance to the children, in which Our Lady revealed Her thorn encircled Heart and from it *rays shone upon the three children causing them "to feel lost in God"* and to exclaim:

"O Most Holy Trinity, I adore Thee! My God, My God, I love Thee in the Most Blessed Sacrament!"

Oh, indeed the Fatima week has just begun! On what day of the remaining week will awareness of this *wonder of God's Love for man* permeate the world?

What wonders of Grace and Mercy there are to come!

CHAPTER FOURTEEN

VIGIL HOUR BECOMES A NIGHT

As The Final Effort Reaches Its Climax

Over three hundred years ago, The Sacred Heart asked so little to do so much! To end the reign of Satan in the world, He asked only that the Church hold before the faithful the sign of His Heart. He asked for consecration to His Heart with frequent Communion, a special Communion of Reparation on First Friday, and for the Feast of the Sacred Heart. And there was one thing more:

He asked for an hour of reparatory prayer before midnight on the vigil of each Friday.

The world was slow in responding. Indeed, how many ever made those holy hours?

Satan's reign not only continued but *increased to the point of militant atheism spreading from an atheist Russia throughout the entire world.*

Then, He came with His Mother to make similar requests of devotion to Her Heart pierced, like His, with thorns.

She promised the conversion of Russia and the triumph of Her Heart. It would become the triumph of the Heart of Her Son.

The "final effort" was reaching its climax.

All In One Night

Altogether in the course of an entire month, *only about six hours* are needed to fulfill all the requests of both Hearts for the Friday vigils and the First Friday and Saturday Communions of Reparation.

Finally moved by the appeal of the Hearts of Jesus and Mary, pierced by our sins, thousands of generous souls have now been inspired to combine all those hours in one night a month, crying out: "**For Your Two Hearts, a night of reparation...from the eve of First Friday to the morning of First Saturday!**"

O, what a wonderful response to their final appeal of Love! How needed! How timely!

Jesus, Who had asked for Communions of Reparation *on the First Friday*, now revealed through Sister Lucia of Fatima:

"The time is coming when the rigor of My Justice will punish the crimes of various nations. Some of them will be annihilated."

Then, appearing with His Mother as She asked for the First Saturday Communions of Reparation, He said:

"*Have pity on the Heart of your most holy Mother*, covered with thorns with which ungrateful men pierce it at every moment, **and there is no one to make an act of reparation** to remove them."

Now those who make the First Saturdays and the vigilers are responding to His great desire. He said:

"I desire that devotion to the Immaculate Heart of My Mother be placed *alongside devotion to My Own Sacred Heart.*"

Almost Perfect Response

An all-night vigil, from the First Friday evening to the First Saturday morning, would seem the almost perfect response to the Hearts of Jesus and Mary for reparation. It seems to fulfill in a special way the wish of Our Lord: "That devotion to the Immaculate Heart of My Mother be placed alongside devotion to My Own Sacred Heart.

Praising these vigils, Pope John XXIII said: "This is the cloister brought into the world!"

Thousands are now making these vigils all around the world. Yet amazingly few even know about them!

Cardinal O'Connor, speaking to vigilers in New York City said: "Very few of those whom the world considers important *would have any idea* that you are here now (making this vigil before the Blessed Sacrament) and will be here through the night. But *Our Lord knows.*"

Yes, He knows.

And His Sacred Heart is consoled, not only by the adoration and the First Friday Communion His Heart asked of us, but also by our response to His plea to have pity on the Heart of His Mother and ours.

Fr. Armand Dasseville, O.F.M. Cap., after leading vigils for twenty five years, explained:

"Night vigilers pray in reparation for the wrongs in society and to obtain special graces and mercy for a generally sinful and sick world... *The vigils identify with Jesus and Mary in the redemption of the world.*"

Leo XIII solemnly consecrated the human race to the Sacred Heart of Jesus on June 11, 1899. (He called this the most importnat act of his Pontificate.) In the imagery of Sister Lucia, this ushered in *the third day* of the messages of the Sacred Heart up to 1917, followed by two world wars and the atomic bomb.

Pope John Paul II, in union with all the bishops of the world, consecrated the world to the Immaculate Heart of Mary on March 25, 1984. In this, he saw "great hope for the world." It ushered in *the third day* of the "week" *of Fatima* which Sr. Lucia said "*has just begun.*"

CHAPTER FIFTEEN

THE PRODIGAL'S HOUR OF REDEMPTION

Gazing at that final vision of Fatima, at the pierced Hearts of Jesus and Mary, we are gazing at co-redemption. That image cries out to us. Our Lady points to Her thorn-pierced heart, pleading with Her children to join Her in offering the passion of Jesus to the Father.

She said at Akita: "*So far I have prevented the coming of calamities* by offering to the Father the sufferings of the Son on the cross, His Precious Blood, *and beloved souls who console Him...*"

When St. Paul says that we make up "for what is lacking in the suffering of Christ," he affirms this mission of co-redemption. Our Lady said at Fatima: "Many souls are lost because there is no one to pray and to make sacrifice for them."

Many souls are lost, and the reign of Satan continues because *we* have failed to respond to this final appeal of love from the pierced Heart of Jesus, pouring His Life out to us in the Eucharist, repeated at Fatima by His Mother.

We begin our response with an act of consecration. We complete it with living our morning offering (aided by Rosary and Scapular) and by First Friday/Saturday vigils.

No Greater Love

In the fourth apparition to St. Margaret Mary (called the "great" apparition), Our Lord said:

"You could not show Me greater love than by doing what I have already demanded of you..."

Then Jesus did for St. Margaret what Our Lady did for the children of Fatima, when they said they would be willing to do whatever she asked. *He showed her His Heart.* And He said:

"Behold this Heart which has so loved men that It spared nothing, even going so far as to exhaust and consume Itself to prove to them It's love. And in return, I receive from the greater part of men nothing but ingratitude, by the contempt, irreverence, sacrileges, and coldness with which they treat Me in this Sacrament of Love. But what is still more painful to Me is that even souls consecrated to Me are acting in this way."

And what Our Lord says of His Sacred Heart, He applies almost word for word, as we shall show shortly, to the Immaculate Heart of His Mother.

If His Heart is pierced with the thorns of ingratitude, and especially by the contempt, irreverence, sacrilege, and coldness with which they treat Him in His Sacrament of Love, so is the Immaculate Heart of Mary who said at Pellevoisin: "What MOST offends my Immaculate Heart are careless Communions."

Is the Heart of Jesus, anxious for so many souls away from God, no longer able to contain It's flames of love? So is the Immaculate Heart of Mary.

Now Is the Critical Hour

And now is the critical hour. More than a billion souls are so far from God that they are no longer even cognizant of their Heavenly Father's House which either they themselves abandoned, or their ancestors abandoned before them. And they face the alternative of nuclear self-destruction if they do not awaken to their plight.

Is it any wonder that, in addition to revealing to us the pleading Hearts of Jesus and Mary, the Father Himself adds His voice at this last hour, calling to His prodigal children?[29]

Will they remain unaware of the desperation of their plight? Will they remain unaware that they need no longer eat the husks of despair? Is there some way to make them know that love and safety waits them in their Father's House?

There is a way.

And there is new hope that it will now succeed.

In the "greatest darkness before the dawn" of this third day of Fatima, the prodigal children of the world, having wasted their spiritual inheritance in riotous living, are reduced to eating the fodder of pigs. It is the moment of mercy, the moment of awakening.

Hour of Hope

Even while saying that the Fatima message is important because it gives the "specific response" needed to meet the

---

[29] We refer especially to the beautiful messages of Mother Eugenia Ravasio which, although approved some fifty years ago, are only now becoming known. For information contact *God the Father Apostolate*, 6111 Steubenville Pike, McKees Rock, PA 15136.

alternative of man's self destruction, the Pope said in the millennial encyclical that he felt called to lead the Church into the new millennium "In the hope of the definitive coming of the Kingdom!"

Why, in this dark hour of almost worldwide violence, abortion, godlessness, and ever present nuclear weapons, does the Pope feel called to speak of "Crossing the threshold of HOPE?"

This is *that* day when the prodigal son, facing the alternative of self-destruction, may realize his plight and return to His Father's House. And it is likely that we shall see the first evidence of this in Russia.

Who will bring it about?

The same few chosen by God to have brought about the dissolution of the Soviet Union in 1990 with the Fatima pledge.

Unrecognized Sign

Jesus said that it was "so my *entire* Church will know" that the change in Russia was brought about through the Immaculate Heart of His Mother (the Fatima event), that He insisted it would take place only when all the bishops of the world made the collegial consecration. On having received this great sign they were to place devotion to the Immaculate Heart of His Mother "alongside devotion to My Own Sacred Heart."

That act by the Pope and all the bishops of the world was a *sine qua non* condition for dissolution of the Soviet Union, so that NOW, following that change in Russia, the entire Church would look to the Heart of Jesus next to the Heart of His Mother.

Bl. Padre Pio had said the change in Russia would come "when there is a Blue Army member for every Communist." It would come (which is equivalent to saying the collegial consecration would take place) only when a sufficient number were fulfilling the basic requests of Our Lady contained in the Fatima pledge.

It happened. But do we, and do the bishops of the world, fully appreciate what has happened, and what brought it about?

A Great Sign

The collegial consecration took place on March 25, 1984. And the following May 13, the day of the first apparition of Fatima, a massive explosion in Russia destroyed two thirds of the weapons of the Soviet northern fleet stockpiled at Sveremosk.

Due to Communist secrecy, the news did not leak out for several weeks. The first release by United Press International was on July 11. It quoted *Jane's Defense Weekly*, a well known civilian intelligence agency in London which reports on world armaments.

Two key Soviet leaders died shortly afterwards. There followed a dramatic change in Soviet leadership with the rise of Gorbachev.

By *December* of 1984, U.S. intelligence was aware that a radical change had taken place in Russia. An agent, who had been monitoring Russian broadcasts for more than thirty years, said that he could not believe what he was hearing as he listened to Soviet radio at that time—only eight months after the collegial consecration.

Pope Speaks of it as a Miracle

Was this not as great a sign from God as the "great sign" of the apparent fire over Europe in 1938?

In the fall of 1993, when the Pope visited the Baltic countries and spoke for the first time in ex-Soviet territory, he said that in the collapse of atheistic Marxism, one can see "the finger of God." He alluded to a "mystery," and even "A MIRACLE," when speaking of the collapse, after seventy years, of a power that seemed as if it would be around for centuries.[30]

But most of the world has failed to recognize this great sign of God's intervention. Most of the world ignores even what a great intervention it was.

Most political experts never thought the Soviet Union would end as it did. It was logical to expect that the Soviet leaders, when the people of Russia rejected failed Communist

---

[30] *Crossing the Threshold of Hope*, pg. 127.

doctrine, would save themselves and Russia by launching a nuclear attack on the West.

This is certainly what they planned when Kruschev pounded the table at the U.N., and said, "We will bury you!"

But just after that event, on October 13, the anniversary of the miracle of Fatima, a super bomb (which the Russians had just developed) exploded, killing most of Russia's top nuclear experts.

And if that were not "sign" enough, as we said above, it was *on May 13*, 1984 that the devastating explosion took place at Sveremosk, only six weeks after the collegial consecration.

Nuclear War Postponed

Is it a surprise that *Jane's Weekly*, quoted above, said that a nuclear war would probably have taken place in 1985? Or that Sister Lucia, who knew nothing of that report, said in the October 1993 interview: "There would have been a nuclear war in 1985."

And who prevented it? Who brought us to the moment of mercy, the moment when the Holy Father and all the

Pope John Paul II speaking with Gorbachev, the Soviet leader largely instrumental in the change in Russia.

bishops of the world finally responded to the request of Our Lord concerning His Heart and the Heart of His Mother?

Our Lady told us at Akita. She said that so far She has been able to hold back the chastisement in two ways:

1) By offering the Passion of her Son to the Father (being intensely now the mediatrix and co-redemptrix at the foot of the Cross);

2) By the cooperation of a few generous souls.

As you read these words do you feel they are meant for *you?* Or, do you just take it for granted that you are too unqualified?

For "Little" People

When St. Margaret Mary was asked by Jesus to make known a message by which He intended to withdraw men from the reign of Satan and to put an end to that reign, she asked:

"But, O Lord, to whom do You address Yourself? To so frail a creature and poor sinner, whose unworthiness might even be capable of preventing the accomplishment of Your designs? You have so many generous souls to carry out Your designs."

"Ah, poor innocent," Jesus replied, "do you not know that I employ those who are weak to confound those who are strong, and that it is usually the poor in spirit to whom I show My power with more splendor, so that they may not ascribe anything to themselves?"

When we get to Heaven, we will be surprised to see how many "unqualified" persons made up that army of spiritual response which finally obtained for us the collegial consecration and the dissolution of the Soviet Union. And they inspired many wonderful priests and bishops to act.

After Jesus insisted that He had chosen St. Margaret Mary, she asked Our Lord to give her the means to carry out His wishes. Our Lord then told her the instrument he had chosen:

"Address yourself to My servant, Fr. Claude de la Colombiere, and tell him from Me to establish this devotion to the best of his ability..."

We repeat these words of Jesus here for two reasons:

1) Most lay persons feel they are inadequate, like St. Margaret Mary;

2) St. Claude de la Colombiere, who was chosen for this mission, had another mission very relevant to the Two Hearts.

In a moment we will speak of the role of the laity. Here, in the light of that "other mission" of St. Claude, we must say a special word about the answer given by Sister Lucia when she was asked why Our Lady held the Scapular in the final vision of Fatima. She said: "It is because, as Pope Pius XII said, *it is the sign of consecration to Her Immaculate Heart. She wants everyone to wear it.*"

It is an important part of the response.

The author's book, *Her Glorious Title,* on the appearance of Our Lady of Mt. Carmel at Fatima and the role of the Scapular in the final effort of the Sacred Hearts to wrest mankind from the reign of Satan.

CHAPTER SIXTEEN

SIGN OF THEIR HEARTS

It was before I heard of Fatima, and six years before my first interview with Sister Lucia, that I wrote the book *Mary in Her Scapular Promise.* Later, I came to know the final vision of Our Lady at Fatima, in which She appeared with the Scapular. Then I renamed the book *Sign of Her Heart.*

But the original title was from the words of St. Claude de la Colombiere: *"In that celebrated (Scapular) promise, Mary reveals all the tenderness of Her Heart."*

The Scapular is the sign of covenant between our hearts and the Immaculate Heart of Mary. God chose St. Claude to preach devotion to the Sacred Heart and inspired him to preach, at the same time, that the surest way to please His Sacred Heart is to be united to the Immaculate Heart of Mary. The saint said that, while there are many signs of devotion to Mary: "I aver without a moment's hesitation that the Scapular is the greatest of all."

There is a very, very important practical side to this.

Bl. José Maria Escriva asked: "What is the first thing necessary for devotion to Mary?" And he answered: *"To realize that She is alive."*

The Need to KNOW

We need to KNOW that Our Lady is listening when we pray. We need to REALIZE we are under Her mantle, next to Her Heart. And St. Claude says: "I need but reach out and *touch the Scapular* and I KNOW."

In a letter to a cousin who was married at Lourdes, St. Therese (the "Little Flower") wrote to the newlyweds that while *the marriage vow made them two in one flesh, the Scapular made them two in one heart because, uniting them under Our Lady's mantle, it united them in Mary's Heart.*

Two Hearts in covenant with the Immaculate Heart of Mary are, in Our Lady's protective love, more deeply in covenant with each other. And *the Scapular is the principal devotion of covenant with Mary.*

St. Claude said: "Since all forms of devotion to Mary cannot be equally agreeable to her I aver, without a moment's hesitation, that the Scapular is the most favored of all. I maintain that there is no devotion which renders our salvation so certain, and none to which we ought to attach ourselves with more confidence and zeal."

This does not mean that the Scapular is better than the Rosary. Sister Lucia said, "The Scapular and the Rosary are inseparable." But it is especially important to be *aware* of Our Lady's presence through Her constant and protecting love. It is important to KNOW when we pray that She is as close as love. She is listening.

St. Claude continues: "I would reproach myself were I to weaken your confidence in those other devotions to Mary, for they are all salutary and cannot fail to touch Her maternal Heart. But, if She graciously accords Her favors through them, how much more propitious will She not be to those who wear Her Scapular."

Paul VI said in application of Par. 67 of *Lumen Gentium* (which mandates that traditional devotions to Our Lady are to be "fostered" in the Church) that the two devotions MOST to be fostered now are the Rosary and the Scapular.[31] These are the two practical means offered by Our Lady of Fatima in God's "final effort" for the triumph of Her Immaculate Heart in individuals and in the world.

The Scapular, like the Rosary, is more than just a physical sign. It is like a religious habit which sets a person apart as *BELONGING to God in a special way.* In the case of the Scapular, that belonging to God in a special way is in covenant with Mary. And when we are in covenant with Mary, *we become at once intimately in covenant with Jesus.*

"My Livery and That of My Son"

Our Lady's very first words at Pellevoisin[32] were addressed to Satan, who had appeared at the deathbed of a dying young woman named Estelle Faguette. Our Lady said to the demon:

"What are you doing here? Do you not see that she is wearing MY LIVERY AND THAT OF MY SON?"

It was the first time in an approved apparition (which is usually an apparition with a public message) that Our Lady identified the Scapular not only as the sign of belonging to Her Heart but also of belonging to the Heart of Her Son. (A livery is a garment which indicates that the one who wears it is in the service of the person whose livery it is.)

Estelle, who had been expected to die within a matter of hours, was cured. (The miracle was recognized by the Church in 1983.) Fifteen apparitions followed in which Our Lady wore a small scapular over Her robe, which had a white front. As mentioned in the previous chapter on the importance of consecration to the Sacred Hearts, the Mother of God invited Estelle to come and kiss the small scapular She was wearing. As Estelle did so, THE SACRED HEART

---

[31] The Pope made the statement through the International Marian Congress reported in *Osservatore Romano, April 2, 1965*: "You will make known our will and our exhortations which we base upon the dogmatic constitution of the Ecumenical Council II, which is in complete conformity with our thought and indeed upon which our thought is based: That one ever hold in great esteem the practices and exercises of the devotion to the Most Blessed Virgin which have been recommended for centuries by the Magisterium of the Church. Among them we judge well to recall especially the Marian Rosary and the religious use of the Scapular of Mount Carmel, a form of piety which is adapted by its simplicity to the spirit indeed of everyone, and is most largely widespread among the faithful for an increase of spiritual fruit."

[32] A French village in the Diocese of Bourges, south of Tours, where Our Lady appeared to Estelle Faguette. The miracle and message were recognized by the Church in an unofficial way with a shrine and annual diocesan pilgrimages, but it was over a hundred years before official recognition was given in 1983.

appeared upon it *as a living Heart. And in that moment, Estelle had a mystical experience of the union of her heart with the Hearts of Jesus and Mary.*

For a more complete understanding of this, the reader is urgently referred to my books *Sign of Her Heart* and especially *Her Glorious Title.* The latter might more appropriately bear the title *The Sacred Hearts Revealed in Our Time.* It speaks extensively of the wonderful message of Pellevoisin and of the revelations in Hungary on the conquering of the world by the "Flame of Love"—the Flame of the united love of the Sacred Hearts.

Spiritual Warfare

There is frequently a tendency, especially among modernists, to minimize the miraculous, and to downplay devotions like the Scapular and the Rosary. Even such great miracles as the parting of the Red Sea are given suggested natural explanations (as has the great miracle of Fatima, even though Our Lady foretold that it would be a MIRACLE, and that it would happen at a pre-announced time and place "so that all may believe").

All do not believe, and unfortunately some who do not believe devise scholarly arguments to shatter the belief of others. And if they cannot shatter belief they can sow doubts.

And in the case of devotions, doubts can be deadly.

The Scapular has been the subject of attack ever since Our Lady first gave it to the world in 1271, even though, after more than seven centuries, it has emerged as one of the two most widespread and most indulgenced devotions in the Church.

Decision of the Pope of the Council

We mentioned above that Pope Paul VI said that, in our time, the Rosary and the Scapular are the two Marian devotions MOST to be promoted in the Church. And the circumstances under which the Pope said this make it especially important.

During months of discussion about Paragraph 67 of *Lumen Gentium* (the Dogmatic Constitution on the Church), the commission debated whether any specific devotion should be mentioned. Some wanted to mention the Rosary. But the commission decided that *it was up to the Pope, at any given moment of history, to indicate which devotions were to be especially promoted and practiced at that time.*

Shortly after Pope Paul VI had signed *Lumen Gentium* in the Vatican Council, this same Pope, in solemn circumstances, declared that of all the devotions to Mary, *two* were urgent at this time: the Scapular and the Rosary.

Those who would belittle these devotions decry "private" revelation. And it is very important to note that although devotions to the Heart of Jesus and to the Heart of Mary have been requested in our time in private revelations, *it is because they are already in public revelation and have weathered centuries of experience, that the Church approves and encourages these devotions.* The effectiveness of the Rosary and the Scapular devotions have been in the Church *more than seven hundred years.*

For us who believe the Church cannot err, especially in the voice of a Church Council or in a pronouncement of the Pope, the attacks on these devotions should be seen for what they are: a part of Satan's effort to destroy them because of their great benefit to souls.[33]

Front Lines of Spiritual Warfare

When we promote the devotion to the Two Hearts, we are in the very front lines of spiritual warfare. St. Margaret Mary said that Jesus told her: "This devotion was the last effort of His Love granted to men in these latter ages in order to withdraw them from the empire of Satan *which He desired to destroy...*"

The Venerable Francis Yepes, brother of St. John of the Cross, was given to know that the three devotions Satan fears most are the invocation of the names of Jesus and of Mary,

---

[33] At the time of the writing of this book, there is a move to deny the Sabbatine Privilege of the Scapular because the original Sabbatine Bull of 1324 has been lost and the validity of copies called into question. However, the privilege stands completely independent of the original bull. It is a type of "indulgence" ratified by several Popes and in particular by Pope Paul VI. See next chapter: *Added Incentive.*

and the wearing of the Scapular. Demons were heard to cry out: "O Scapular, how many souls you snatch from us!"

They were actually saying: "O Hearts of Jesus and Mary, how many souls YOU snatch from us! *What power do we have over souls consecrated to Your Hearts!?*"

We have said before that this has special significance to the family. It is a *continuing sign* (night and day, in every

Over 2,000 bishops gathered in St. Peter's in the second Vatican Coucil. They insisted on traditional devotions to Our Lady, of which, said the Pope, especially needed today are the Rosary and the Scapular.

moment) of spiritual bond among members of a family. It is *the sign that all its members are in covenant with the Immaculate Heart of Mary* and therefore, of course, with the Heart of Jesus.

What a consolation it is when someone we love is clothed in the Scapular at the moment of death!

The Great Promise

It was not our intention to speak here at any greater length of the Scapular except for the Sabbatine Privilege. We will explain this in the next chapter because this is a "special incentive" to fulfill the basic requests of Our Lady of Fatima.

But a special incident in the life and writings of St. Claude seems to clamor for attention here.

He tells of a woman who jumped into the river to commit suicide. The Scapular (which bears the promise that whoever dies clothed in it will die in the state of Grace) floated like a life preserver, holding her up.

A man fishing in the river saw her and went to the rescue, but before he reached her she snatched off the Scapular and sank out of sight.[34]

It has never been known, in over seven hundred years, that anyone who died in the Scapular died refusing grace. The example above is exceptional because normally a person who wants to remain in sin will not continue to wear the Scapular. Indeed, this author's introduction to the Scapular at the age of five was from a similar incident with a very different ending.

A companion of my father was seized with a paralyzing fit while swimming in a dangerous river. My father saw his struggling companion held up by the scapular as if by a life preserver. But this time it was a soul preserver. The boy confessed that he was in mortal sin and realized that, because he was wearing that sign of Our Lady's maternal love, he was saved. He changed his life.

---

[34] Vol. iv, Sermons de La Colombiere, Edition of Clermont Ferrand, 1884. Cf Milagros y Prodigios del Santo Escapulario, Fernandes Martin, Madrid, 1956, pg. 62.

Chapter Seventeen

ADDED INCENTIVE

It may seem a slight diversion from our main theme, but it seems necessary to write here of the Sabbatine Privilege, which modernists and others tend to put aside at a time when it can be a tremendous incentive to fulfill the essential requests of Fatima: *chastity according to one's state with use of the Rosary and the Scapular.*

Pope Pius XI called the Sabbatine Privilege "**Our greatest privilege from the Mother of God which extends even after death...**"

This privilege, first promulgated by Pope John XXII and subsequently ratified by many other Popes, promises *freedom from Purgatory soon after death*, especially on the First Saturday.

Three Conditions

In 1324, when this "super indulgence" was first promulgated, the conditions were three: 1) Chastity according to one's state of life; 2) the Scapular; 3) the Little Office of the Blessed Virgin or, if one could not read, fasting on Wednesdays and Fridays.

All priests have the faculty to enroll in the Scapular and to commute the third condition to some other prayer or work.

In 1950, the Blue Army of Our Lady of Fatima asked Rome to substitute the Rosary for the third condition. Rome said that since Blue Army members were required to wear the Scapular and to say the Rosary, a request could be included on the Blue Army membership pledge to substitute the Rosary for the third condition for all its members.[35]

That meant that *for fulfilling the basic requests of Our Lady of Fatima, one could obtain this great privilege.*

It would almost seem that this was scheduled in the plans of Providence because the first and most important condition for response to the message of Fatima is avoidance of sin. "Men must stop offending God," said Our Lady. "He is already too much offended." *And Our Lady also said: "More souls are lost because of sins of impurity."*

And the primary condition for the Sabbatine Privilege is chastity according to one's state in life.

Blessed Gifts of Our Mother!

Being a practical mother at Fatima, Our dearest Mother placed this primary condition in a *positive* form: She asked for *the sanctification of our daily duties.* And this is done quite simply by making the Morning Offering of the sacrifices needed to avoid temptation, with the two aids She offers: The Scapular and the Rosary.

Our loving, Heavenly Mother had already been encouraging us along this simple way of holiness for almost seven hundred years through the Sabbatine Privilege. It is a way which greatly facilitates God's final effort to draw us from the reign of Satan.

With its three simple conditions, this privilege offers us the assurance that we shall be saints *before we die.* How else could we be freed from Purgatory by the first Saturday after death *if we had not by then become holy?*

St. Alphonsus, Doctor of the Church, went so far as to say that if we do **a little more** than what is required for the Sabbatine Privilege, "**may we not hope that we will not go to Purgatory AT ALL?**" And, forty years after the death of the saint, his Brown Scapular was found perfectly preserved midst the corruption of everything else in his tomb.

Pere Lamy, who saw the coming triumph of the Immaculate Heart of Mary, said: "As for Our Lady, Her

---

35 A note is usually appended to the Blue Army pledge with a box to be checked because each person, on joining the Blue Army, must make the request. This is required because the Rosary is not the only possible substitution.

kindness gets Her everywhere... *The Blessed Virgin said again to me one day that* **those who have fulfilled the conditions of Her Sabbatine Privilege will be drawn out of Purgatory by Her on the first Saturday after death.**"

How Precious!

This was said in 1924, not long after Pope St. Pius X had given permission for the use of the Scapular medal adding, in the papal decree, *"not excluding the Sabbatine Privilege."* The Pope gave this permission for serious reasons, such as conditions in the trenches during the first World War. Pere Lamy said:

"How precious then is the Brown Scapular which brings us deliverance from such places of pain, for Purgatory is extremely painful. The Blessed Virgin told me that She thought it better to stay behind 15 years, dragging one's weight on earth, than to spend 15 minutes in Purgatory."

Also, we may remark: How precious is the virtue of chastity!—the one virtue which is the prime condition for obtaining this great privilege.

One of the strongest motives for wearing the Scapular (with an understanding that it is a sign of *our consecration to the Immaculate Heart* of Mary) is that it is a great aid and safeguard for this beautiful virtue, especially when combined with the Rosary. Indeed, it has been said: "No one can wear the Scapular and say the fifteen decades of the Rosary daily with attention to the mysteries and remain in mortal sin."[36]

God's Final Effort Provides These Great Aids

And falling into sin does not bar us from this great privilege.

The condition of the Sabbatine Privilege (that we observe chastity according to our state of life) does not mean that if we commit a sin against chastity, we will lose the privilege. If we *have a sincere intention not to sin,* we are fulfilling

---

[36] This was the opinion of St. Grignion de Montfort. See the author's book *Sex and the Mysteries.*

the Sabbatine condition. We need merely go to confession and start again with that sincere intention.

The power of the Scapular and Rosary is to keep us in that sincere intention.

By the Scapular, we are consecrated to the Immaculate Heart of Mary. As we wear it, the strings over our shoulders are like Our Lady's arms protecting us. The panel over our hearts symbolizes being beneath Her powerfully protecting mantle.

And when we pray the Rosary with awareness of this, we drive evil away. Sins against chastity become abhorrent. And if we should be snared by them, we will fly to confession. Thus we become saints, rejoicing in those words of the great Marian Doctor:

"And, if we do a little more than Our Lady asks...can we not hope that we will not go to Purgatory at all?"

Stop and think of that for a moment. Remember that it was said by a doctor of the Church. Remember he is canonized, and in the midst of the corruption of everything else in his tomb his Brown Scapular was miraculously preserved and is to be seen in perfect condition to this day. Then, consider this:

Certainly a "little more" than asked for the Sabbatine Privilege *is the devotion of the five First Saturdays.*[37] Indeed, they remind us of this great privilege which is often called simply: *The First Saturday Privilege.*

---

[37] In the interview on October 11, 1993, Sister Lucia said Our Lady wants *all the conditions of the pledge* but that especially now, in what she called the "post consecration phase" of Fatima, Our Lady asks for the devotion of the five First Saturdays. See *Duas Entrevistas com a Irma Lucia* published at Fatima by Regina Press, May 1998.

CHAPTER EIGHTEEN

PRIVILEGED TIME

How privileged we are to live in these "latter times" when the Sacred Heart of Jesus, in union with the Immaculate Heart of His Mother, will draw men from the empire of Satan and destroy it.

It is the time when His Sacred Heart has "entrusted the peace of the world to Her" (Blessed Jacinta). It is the time of the promised triumph.

St. John Bosco had a vision of this time. He saw the bark of Peter tossed in a terrible storm and the Pope valiantly guiding it towards two pillars: on one the Eucharist and the other Our Lady—the pillars of the Two Hearts.

Appearing as a Queen, crowned and sceptered, with Her Son holding the globe of the world, She promised a victory before the year 2000, which would be "greater than the victory of Lepanto."

That victory took place on the feast of Her Queenship in 1990 with the dissolution of the Soviet Union.

Now the Church makes it way through the storm towards the pillars of the Two Hearts confident of victory.

But the storm seems to intensify. How bad may it get? How long may it last?

Was the Apostolate Over

With an apology for speaking personally, it was on May 2, the day of the beatification of Bl. Padre Pio, that I began to write this book as I asked myself the question:

With all the evil in the world today, and with so little interest in Fatima, is the Blue Army, of which Bl. Padre Pio was the spiritual father, a thing of the past? I was asking the question not only because of the decline in interest in Fatima but because of adversities in the apostolate itself, as I have already said in the foreword of this book.

And, if I am not mistaken, Bl. Padre Pio had me ask another question: "If Sister Lucia says that the Fatima week has just begun, has not the world apostolate just begun?"

Immediately the thought came: "Look at Fatima in the context of history."

I had often thought of the comparison made by Our Lord beween the failure to respond to the message of Fatima and the failure to respond to the message of His Sacred Heart. Finally, it stunned me. Invoking Bl. Padre Pio, I began that same day to write this book.

I was later very impressed to learn that the miraculous liquefaction of the blood of St. Januarius, which for hundreds of years had occurred on May 1st, had not happened this year until the same May 2, at 11:30, when Bl. Padre Pio was beatified.

Bl. Padre Pio's Message

Half a million people spilled out of St. Peter's square that day (May 2, 1999), and another half a million spilled over the square in front of St. John Lateran to watch the ceremny on a giant television screen. In living memory, no beatification (or even canonization) like this had ever taken place in Rome.

Did those hundreds of thousands know that before leaving this world, Bl. Padre Pio had provided a way that those after his death could still become his spiritual children? They could do so in just one way: *they could make the Blue Army pledge* (the basic requests of Our Lady: Morning Offering, Scapular and Rosary).

Asked one day whether it was a good thing to belong to the Blue Army, Bl. Padre Pio answered: *"Could you do anything better?"*

Special Memories

Since this is probably my last book, please bear with me for sharing a few memories of this unusual saint, who understood better than most people of our time the wonder and power of devotion to the Two Hearts.

I had the great good fortune to have seen Bl. Padre Pio some twenty-five times over the years, and even of serving his Mass. One incident I especially recall concerned a crucifix which gave off a perfume after he blessed it. Another concerned the wounds in his feet. Others concerned Garabandal and a book I was writing on the Eucharist. But perhaps the most extraordinary incident concerned Bl. Padre Pio's role as Spiritual Father of the Blue Army, and the International Pilgrim Virgin statue of Our Lady of Fatima.

This was a special statue of Our Lady, blessed at Fatima on May 13, 1947, to be carried across Europe to Russia. It was called the "Pilgrim Virgin." Miracles took place causing Pope Pius XII to exclaim:

"In 1946, I crowned Our Lady at Fatima as Queen of the World and the following year, through the Pilgrim Virgin, She set forth as though to claim Her dominion. And the favors She performs along the way are such that we can scarcely believe what we are seeing with our eyes."

When the same Pope instituted the feast of the Queenship of Mary in St. Peter's in Rome in 1954, His Holiness said: "I first crowned Her Queen at Fatima." He referred to the statue as "The Messenger of Her Royalty."

Bl. Padre Pio's Cure

When the Pilgrim Virgin visited San Giovanni Rotondo, where Bl. Padre Pio lived, the saintly priest was bedridden with so severe an illness that the word "hopeless" was used. For some time, he had not been able to say Mass. And, for Bl. Padre Pio that was a much greater suffering than any illness, even greater than the wounds he bore in hands, feet, and side for fifty years.

A vast crowd had come to San Giovanni for the visit of the statue. An aerial photo of the occasion shows thousands of people overflowing the square and filling the approaches in every direction.

It was at the end of the visit that the wonder took place.

The helicopter bearing the statue was flying off to the north when suddenly it banked around and flew back to hover beside the monastery. "Help me," Bl. Padre Pio said to the friars in the room. And they helped him from the bed to the window.

"Little Mother!" Bl. Padre Pio exclaimed, "When you came, I was like this (ill, unable to say Mass). Do you leave me this way?"

Instantly he was cured. He was able to say Mass from then until he died (September 23, 1968).

Behind the Story

The above facts have been told in almost all the books about Bl. Padre Pio and in the film *Fifty Years of Thorns and Roses*. The mayor of San Giovanni, who was a lifelong friend of Bl. Padre Pio, said this cure by Our Lady stood out in his mind above all the other events in Bl. Padre Pio's life, other than the stigmata.

God could have prevented the illness of Bl. Padre Pio, which doctors thought would end in his death. He could have cured him in many ways. But God willed to make this dramatic statement about Our Lady of Fatima.

There is a surprising story behind the story which has never been told. The priest in the helicopter was Msgr. Giovanni Strazzacappa who had founded the Blue Army in Italy. He told me what happened.

The pilot suddenly swirled the machine around. In surprise, Monsignor asked what was happening. The pilot, himself surprised, said he just felt "compelled" to turn around. Then to the amazement of both, they saw Bl. Padre Pio come to the window with the help of his friars and cry out to Our Lady. But this is still not the end of the story.

A Statue for a Crucifix

Bl. Padre Pio had long had a special devotion to Our Lady of Fatima. He made the prophecy: "Russia will be converted when there is a Blue Army member for every Communist." He had accepted all who make and keep the Blue Army pledge as his spiritual children (for whom he will wait at the gates of Heaven "until all have entered"). In gratitude for the great favor through the Pilgrim statue of Our Lady of Fatima, Bl. Padre Pio sent *a crucifix* to the Bishop of

Fatima (the Most Rev. John Venancio) who was the international spiritual head of the Blue Army.

In return for the crucifix, also in recognition of the great favor She had conferred on the world's "living crucifix," *the bishop had a special statue of Our Lady of Fatima* made for Bl. Padre Pio, and gave myself and Msgr. Strazzacappa the privilege of taking it to him.

With a group of Blue Army members, I took the statue by ship from Portugal to Naples, where we were joined by an Italian group led by Msgr. Strazzacappa. With the statue sometimes in one bus and sometimes in another, we prayed our way across Italy to deliver this precious gift to the world beloved Capuchin friar.

When Bl. Padre Pio received the statue, it seemed he was receiving Our Lady Herself. When he bent to kiss the feet of the statue there was a holy silence. I think it was a moment of special meaning to Msgr. Strazzacappa (one of the most gifted and holy priests I have ever known) because of something personal Bl. Padre Pio said to him just after kissing the statue. (He seemed in perfect health, but died unexpectedly a few months later.)

Bl. Padre Pio had the statue *placed over his vesting table in the sacristy*, greeting Her before he went out to say Mass, and on his return. It is featured in the film *Fifty Years of Thorns and Roses.*

The Crucifix

Bl. Padre Pio has been called the "living crucifix" because wounds on his hands and feet and side bled for fifty years. One day, in the hope that he might kiss a crucifix I had purchased, I placed it next to the kneeler where he said his thanksgiving after Mass.

With Jesus still present beneath his heart, the stigmatic priest reached for the crucifix and kissed it with loving devotion.

I retrieved it immediately after he rose from his thanksgiving. To my amazement, it was giving off a most beautiful fragrance. Men in the sacristy crowded about as the fragrance spread. They all wanted to kiss it. "Oh, how fortunate you are!" I heard from one side and another.

I was on my way upstairs into the monastery to speak to Bl. Padre Pio about Garabandal. Several of the men followed me—or I should rather say followed the fragrance flowing from the crucifix I was carrying and jealously guarding (it now hangs in my bedroom with a picture of Bl. Padre Pio kissing it).

Garabandal

I always had a special devotion to Our Lady of Mount Carmel, and I wondered about the authenticity of the reported visions of Her at Garabandal, Spain.

I had met Joey Lomangino and I was convinced that he would not lie or even exaggerate. He said that Bl. Padre Pio had told him to go to Garabandal. There he learned that, by a miracle, he would one day give witness to the apparitions of Our Lady of Mt. Carmel, and he has spread the news all over the world.

Because I was cofounder of the Blue Army, which had a policy of not speaking of unapproved apparitions, I had never gone. Should I?

Bl. Padre Pio gave me two answers. Both were affirmative. I was to obey the Blue Army policy, but I could take a pilgrimage to Garabandal at the time of the miracle.

I marveled (and do so repeatedly to this day) that Bl. Padre Pio did this in such a way as to make clear that he was not anticipating the judgment of the Church. Now, I am no longer an official of the Blue Army and therefore free to go.

To Draw Them to Our Hearts

By now it is well known in most of the world that Our Lady appeared at Garabandal as Our Lady of Mount Carmel but not clothed in the traditional way, in the Carmelite habit. But she always appeared with the small scapular on her wrist or in her hand, the sign by which millions around the world are consecrated to Her Immaculate Heart.

She is reported to have appeared many times, and to have said many words. Much of Her message was similar to what She said at Akita. She spoke of a warning and a miracle. But what was the main reason for all these visions and messages? She Herself told us: "*I have come **for all my children** with the desire of bringing them **to Our Hearts**.*"

I would like to end on those words. They say it all. And I hope I will not detract from their importance by mentioning one other special memory of Bl. Padre Pio.

The Book

His greatest devotions were Our Lady and the Eucharist —the two pillars of the Two Hearts. He almost always had a Rosary in his hand as though clinging to it he was clinging to the hand of his heavenly Mother. And when he said Mass, you were *there* on Calvary.

I decided to write a book on the Eucharist such as had never been written before. It was to be a book which would convince even non-believers. I felt compelled because the Eucharist is at the center of the revelations of Fatima. But I felt unworthy.

So I asked practically every pious soul I met to pray for this intention. I asked daily communicants to remember this intention daily until the book was finished. Some two hundred did so—and it took several years!

But each time I asked Bl. Padre Pio about this, he seemed to ignore me. He usually gave some sign of approval or disapproval. But on this, nothing. I felt sad and concerned, but I went ahead and the book was finally published. Within two years it sold over 100,000 copies.

Only some years later, I learned from a priest who saw Bl. Padre Pio frequently that one day the holy (and now beatified) friar said: "He asks me to pray for that book on the Eucharist. It will have some success in his lifetime, but its greatest success will be after his death."[38]

I thought I should hurry up and die, but apparently I still had *this* book to write about the final unfolding of devotion of the Two Hearts and how and to what extent each of us must be involved in God's final effort to wrest us from the empire of Satan. And Bl. Padre Pio inspired it.

---

[38] For an extraordinary story of Padre Pio, called by one of his fellow Capuchins the spiritual *Founder of the Blue Army*, see my book *The Day I Didn't Die*, pgs. 64-66.

CHAPTER NINETEEN

THE CROSS AND THE TWO HEARTS

Following the inspiration on the day of Bl. Padre Pio's beatification, we have looked at the message of Fatima in the context of history, focusing specifically on the history of the messages of the Two Hearts.

As was said by the teacher of history quoted earlier, we find nothing of those messages in our history books, but all our recent history is explained by them.

The remaining big question is: What are we going to do? More specifically: What will ordinary lay Catholics do when they come to the realization that it is up to them to take the initiative?

The Two Hearts Medal

Before coming to that most important question, there is one last look we should take at the history of the Two Hearts.

Louis XVI went to the guillotine in 1789, just one hundred years after the requests of the Sacred Heart. Now Paris was to become the hatchery of a world atheistic revolution, and, in 1824, Our Lady appeared there on Ferry Street (Rue du Bac). She asked that a medal be struck with an image of *the Two Hearts surmounted by a cross* and surrounded by twelve stars. It came to be known as the miraculous medal.

Perhaps we may come to call it the Two Hearts medal.

The opposite side shows Our Lady dispensing rays of graces upon the world. Around Her are the words: "O Mary, conceived without sin, pray for us who have recourse to you." Beneath Her heel, She crushes the head of a serpent.

Dogma of the Two Hearts

The message of the Two Hearts began to glimmer in the 13th century and was growing brighter and brighter at the time of St. John Eudes and St. Margaret Mary Alacoque. Finally, it began to shed its great light of hope at Fatima and in the revelations of Our Lady of All Nations in Amsterdam (which, after more than 50 years, were approved on May 31, 1996).

Our Lady appeared in Amsterdam as She had in Paris, with Her hands extended, dispensing floods of grace upon the world. Represented on the globe as vast flocks of various colored sheep were the peoples of all nations. She asked us to pray that Our Lord would send NOW His Holy Spirit over the earth. She said that when the Church defined as a dogma that She is co-redemptrix and mediatrix, the triumph would take place.

That dogma could be called the dogma of the Two Hearts.

We said earlier that saints have spoken of the Hearts of Jesus and Mary as one. But they are not equal. One is human, the other Divine. Mary is the co-redemptrix, mediatrix, advocate. And when we understand those titles, we understand the relationship of the Two Hearts.

The Cross

A symbol of Their union is the Cross.

At Amsterdam, Our Lady appeared standing in front of the Cross. At Akita, appearing in the same manner, Our Lady spoke terrible words of warning, at this late hour, if the messages of the Sacred Hearts continue to be ignored.

Also, in the very first apparition to St. Margaret Mary, the Sacred Heart was surmounted by a cross: "The Divine Heart was shown to me as on a throne of flames, more dazzling than the sun and transparent as crystal, with that adorable wound and *surrounded by a crown of thorns*, signifying the pricks caused to It by our sins. *Above, there was a cross*, which meant that from the first moment of His Incarnation, that is, as soon as the Sacred Heart was formed, the cross was planted in It, and that It was filled at once with all the bitterness which humiliation and poverty, and pains and scorn, which His Sacred Humanity was to suffer throughout all His lifetime and in His Sacred Passion."

The Same Cross, the Same Love

When one gazes at this vision of the Sacred Heart and at the vision of the Immaculate Heart at Fatima, *one seems to be gazing at the same Heart.*

Our Lord said the cross was planted in His Heart from the moment of His Incarnation. In like manner, Our Lady has revealed that from that same moment of the Incarnation, illumined by the Holy Spirit that the Child just conceived would die on a cross, she began to feel the piercing sword seen by Simeon—a sword which plunged deeper and deeper with every passing day until Her heart was pierced through at the foot of the cross itself.

The more one looks at the cross, the more one understands the mystery of the Sacred Hearts of Jesus and Mary as the Hearts of the new Adam and the new Eve undoing the sin of our first parents.

But what we often fail to see is that *WE are called to that cross* where St. John the Evangelist represented us. We are called to share in co-redemption. *The Sacred Hearts call to us to help* **make reparation for the sins of men.**

We may shy away from this call as we would shy away from suffering, but that is a deceit of Satan. *We are not asked to suffer any more than daily life demands.* We are asked only to sanctify our daily doings. This is the basic request in the message of Fatima.

Chasm of Realization

What could be called "the extra" asked of us is to make the Communions of Reparation. They have greater reparatory power than all other acts of our entire lives.

Our first call to the foot of the cross is to Holy Mass, consummated in us in Holy Communion. Unfortunately, most believe this but few realize it.

Bl. Padre Pio said the value of the Mass is beyond our imagining. And perhaps the greatest blessing of this stigmatic priest to our age is that he SHOWED this in his wounds and as he actually suffered in pronouncing the words of consecration.

But even the average good person has difficulty in crossing the chasm of "realization," the chasm between seeing and *really* believing.

We may cross it at special moments—special moments of illumination or special moments of spiritual "contact," such as touching the rock on which Our Lady stood at Lourdes, or coming out of the baths of Lourdes and being suddenly dry.

But, we should be able to cross that chasm every time we pray, and especially in the miracle of every Mass and Communion.

Bl. Padre Pio's Wounds

Above, I mentioned that one of my personal special memories of Bl. Padre Pio concerned his wounds.

At first, I had difficulty accepting the miracle of his wounds. I saw the blood on his hands, but everything about him was so very human, so very natural. Even the fragrance from his wounds, and even the fragrance from the crucifix he had kissed, did not seem miraculous but just remarkable. There is a big chasm between belief and realization.

I crossed that chasm with Bl. Padre Pio in an extraordinary encounter.

I had no reason for being there. It was an almost unforgivable intrusion (although, may I say in my defense, not one altogether my fault).

With a man from San Giovanni, I was searching for Bl. Padre Pio and we were told he was "downstairs." So we went down to the cellar (which, if I remember rightly, had a packed dirt floor) and opened first one door, and then another. And there, looking up in surprise at the intrusion, Bl. Padre Pio was seated on a stool, and two friars were bathing the wounds on his feet.

In that brief moment, several impressions swept over me.

First, there was the humility of Bl. Padre Pio and the reverence of the friars, his brothers in the monastery. It was reverence for the mystery—for the bleeding wounds of Jesus which they were bathing.

Bl. Padre Pio's own fellow friars, the priests living with him day after day in the same community, could not be mistaken. Their reverence for Bl. Padre Pio as a "living crucifix" became my moment of realization.

And I recalled that Bl. Padre Pio seemed to suffer from the moment he left the sanctuary to go to the altar to celebrate Mass. I remembered he once said, as though reading my mind as I saw this: "But do you think these wounds are decorations?"

God gave us Bl. Padre Pio to SHOW us the identity of the Mass with Calvary—that the very moment of Jesus dying on the cross becomes *present* to us. We are privileged to stand with Our Lady at the foot of that cross and offer the *infinite* merits of the sacrifice in union with Her Immaculate Heart and then to join in its consummation in the great wonder of Holy Communion.

Their Hearts ask a Communion of Reparation only twice a month. And, They promise that if enough Communions of Reparation are made, the reign of Satan will be brought to an end.

Shared Reparation

As explained in more detail in my book *NOW the Woman Shall Conquer*, the primary message both in Amsterdam and in Akita is that we are to share in the sufferings of the cross.

This was shown by a bleeding wound which appeared on the statue in Akita and on the hand of the nun to whom Our Lady appeared. And in Amsterdam, when Our Lady would move slightly from the front of the cross, the visionary was struck with pain shared from the cross.

As was said above: Do not be frightened. We are not asked to add to our sufferings. *We are asked only to accept and to sanctify them.*

This is the very heart of the message of Fatima. "*Will you be WILLING,*" was the first question Our Lady put to the children, "*to accept* **whatever God will send you** *and to offer it up in reparation for sin and for the conversion of sinners*?"

It took nothing more than a simple "Yes," and immediately, the children were bathed in light from Our Lady's Heart, causing them to "feel lost in God."

Oh, how much suffering is wasted! How much each of us, each day, wastes the precious gold of offering up even small disappointments, contradictions, even inconvenience which, if *offered to Their Hearts becomes as tons of gold for the ransom of souls.*

If only more persons realized the power of the Morning Offering!—offering to the Sacred Heart of Jesus, in union with the Immaculate Heart of our Mother, all God asks of us in our few waking hours—in reparation for our sins and the sins of the world.

That simple practice, made so easy by Our Lady's gifts of Scapular and Rosary, can make saints and change the world.

Chapter Twenty

WHO WILL DO IT?

The requests of Their Hearts are so simple to fulfill, and the rewards are so great! Yet who will persuade the world to respond?

Heaven itself has told us. The answer MUST come from the laity. "The clergy are too few," Our Lady said in Amsterdam. "Mobilize the laity."

It was only when the laity acted, after two hundred years of disaster for France and the world, that the requests of the Sacred Heart began to be heard.

Mandate of the Vatican Council

This is not a reflection on the clergy. It is, according to the second Vatican Council, God's Will in our time as expressed in the Vatican documents and in the Pope's 181-page apostolic exhortation *Christifideles Laici*, which cries out: "You, too, go into My vineyard!"

Often spontaneously, through the power and light of the Holy Spirit, the laity are responding to that cry in ever-increasing numbers.[39]

Following are some examples of lay involvement in the life of the Church today. What is said in a paragraph might fill a book.

---

[39] In the United States, in 1996, the Lay Apostolate Foundation began a series of annual five day retreats for lay apostles. During these retreats, *much of the time was left open for the Holy Spirit—* and sharing. The participating priests said they found the vitality of the laity simply amazing. For information contact LAF, PO Box 50, Asbury, NJ 08802.

We ask the reader to inquire after each paragraph: Are the Sacred Hearts asking too much of *me*?

Anatol Kazczuk was a prisoner in Russia for a year. Just before he expected to be executed, an officer to whom he had spoken of God arranged to set him free. He risked his life to return to Poland where he founded the Blue Army and the Legion of Mary. Subsequently, through a Rosary crusade, he opened the door of Poland for the Pope's first visit.

He Made the Sacrifice

Like many apostles, and like almost all the beatified or canonized lay saints, Anatol wanted to give himself entirely to God when he escaped from the Russian prison camp. He became a Dominican novice in Great Britain. When he learned of the Legion of Mary, he thought: "Oh, how Poland needs this apostolate!" Although he trembled to think of going back behind the Iron Curtain, he made the sacrifice. The rest is history.

Anatol Kazczuk being greeted by the Pope.

If we began to give examples of Lay Apostles around the world, this book would not be large enough. Some lay persons, like Anatol in Poland, and Howard Dee in the Philippines, have had a major impact in their nations which has rippled through the world. We have many examples in the United States of almost heroic proportions.

Maureen Flynn, while a mother of two little children, began to help in a pro-life clinic. When she had no money and needed space, she prayed that, if God wanted her apostolate, He would help. Almost at once, large offices in a new building were offered to her free.

Maureen and her husband, while raising their own large family, developed one of the biggest pro-life centers in America. They came to realize that "ultimate victory depends upon prayer." Today, she and her husband run one of the most successful apostolates in America, with publications (magazine *Signs of the Times*) and videos (Maxkol Productions).

Lay Saints

One of the greatest examples of lay involvement in the life of the church is Blessed Anne Marie Taigi, the amazing mother of seven who was beatified as "the model for young women and mothers." Soon also, we may expect the beatification of the parents of St. Therese, Louis and Zelie Martin, of whom St. Therese said: "I have parents more worthy of Heaven than of earth."

Half a dozen lay apostles have recently been raised to the altars. Yet most laypersons continue to feel that holiness is to be sought only in religious life or the priesthood. They do not see themselves as called to be "apostles," in the lay state, to assist in God's final effort to wrest mankind from Satan's reign.

Jan Connell, author of five books, is a lawyer, a mother, and a grandmother. She has become one of the major lay apostles of our time having founded several of the US Centers for Peace. An apparition at Fatima of Blessed Franciso early in her married life opened her to the supernatural.

Has the reader felt perhaps like St. Margaret Mary: "But I am nobody. Jesus, You make a mistake to count on me!"?

Sometimes God works a wonder to convince us. Sometimes just a sermon, a conversation, a video like that which led to the "conversion" of Kevin Morely, founder of the apostolate for the Triumph of the Immaculate Heart of Mary in Australia. Or it could be a book like this one.

It was on a pilgrimage that Dr. Rosalie Turton experienced the urgency of the Fatima message and decided "to be in the front line of Our Lady's Army." She sold her house and founded the very successful 101 Foundation with pilgrimages, books, videos, and a newsletter reaching tens of thousands.

Dr. Tom Petrisko

Dr. Tom Petrisko runs the Pittsburgh Center for Peace, and has published "newspapers" by the millions on the messages of Our Lady, and on the Eucharist. He has written six books and is actively on the cutting edge of today's spiritual warfare. He gave up a large practice to work as a full time lay apostle.

Likewise, Judge Daniel Lynch gave up his law practice to work full time for Christ the King, and for pro-life especially through Our Lady of Guadalupe. He likens the evil engulfing the world to black asphalt which seems to choke out the good. Like the Holy Father, he sees hope as more and more lay apostles are springing up "like dandelions pushing up through the asphalt." He himself is an inspiring example. Speaking all over America, he calls for the threefold response of consecration, reparation, and adoration.

A sure sign that this explosion of lay vitality is the work of the Holy Spirit is that they all are trying to shake the world with the same message: the response to the requests of the Hearts of Jesus and Mary.

One of the most amazing of these "lay apostles" (which indeed is what they are!) is Bud MacFarland Sr. with eleven children and thirty grandchildren and a major job in a large company. He began his apostolate with a little business card which said "Marian Speaker." He is today the most-in-demand lecturer on the Two Hearts in the country.

Going on NOW

With the exception of the saints mentioned above, these are all examples of people living at the dawn of the third millennium. Each of us might ask: *"Are they people different from me?"*

One of the most amazing stories is that of the foundress of Daughters of Zion. She had a dying husband, six children, a business with nine employees, and she herself became grievously ill. It would have seemed impossible that she could feel a calling to found a major apostolate, one which is now flourishing, and is welcomed by bishops wherever it spreads, producing untold good.

Lena Licata, a housewife and beautician in Fort Lauderdale, Florida, organized Rosary groups in homes for the elderly with amazing results. "We witness the power of this prayer," she testified. "A visitor to one of these Rosary groups was healed of cancer. Can we imagine what healing is being obtained for *souls*?"

We could list dozens who have become involved in the Lay Apostolate Foundation, like Bob and Celeste Behling. Age and limitations of time seem to make no difference.

Produced TV Programs

Julia Ceravolo, who for years had taught CCD classes and had lived the *totus tuus* consecration, applied to the local cable company for time on TV, after hearing a Protestant evangelical deny Our Lady. She proceeded to produce a whole series of programs, most of which appeared on EWTN. She says: "Daily communicants, living their consecration to Our Lady, can do *anything*."

Theresa Gleason, who founded an apostolate for nurses, points out that *an apostolate can be a part of your present vocation.*

Tom Fahy is now a full-time apostle as postulator of the cause of Luisa Picaretta. He is a leader in the apostolate of the Divine Will, which is of MAJOR importance.

Bud MacFarland's son, Bud MacFarland Jr., made a few copies of a tape of one of his father's talks on the apparitions of Our Lady. He began to get requests for more copies. He gave them away free. Soon, he was making them by the hundred. Offerings came in. When he decided to quit his job and produce audio tapes on Our Lady's messages, his father reminded him of the need to support his family. But so much good was being accomplished that, trusting in God, he quit his job and launched what is now the largest Catholic tape apostolate in the world. He also launched *CatholiCity*, a popular Web site with 100,000 "hits" annually on the Internet.

Bud gives space to other apostolates. Dan Lyons gives away a 1,000 rosaries a month through this website, and promotes the youth magazine *Hearts Aflame*. The Internet offers opportunities to thousands for apostleship from their own homes. Many also use e-mail. Others use faxes. Perhaps most useful of all are copying machines, making letter size sheets cheaper than the cost of mailing them. Many duplicate leaflets. Sheets for names to place in Our Lady's Heart are multiplied in this way by name-gatherers.

Vigil Apostles and Vox Populi

One of the most timely movements is sponsored by the Missionary Brothers of the Alliance of the Two Hearts. They enlist and train laity in the door-to-door enthronement of the Sacred Hearts in the home and in the conduct of the First Friday/Saturday vigils. They will go anywhere to help start a vigil. They can be contacted at PO Box 357, Dover, Delaware, 19903.

Another major apostolate now involving thousands of lay apostles is *Vox Populi*, the worldwide campaign to petition the dogma requested by Our Lady of All Nations. In a meeting with the Pope, on July 31, 1999, its founder and director, Dr. Mark Miravalle, S.T.D., was able to give the Holy Father an update *of over 550 Bishops, 42 Cardinals, and nearly six million petitions from over 70 countries.*

Obviously, this is too important to pass over in a few words. In the Church approved apparitions at Amsterdam, Our Lady said that the triumph of Her Immaculate Heart would begin with the proclamation of this dogma. It is explained at length in my book *Now the Woman Shall Conquer.*

Millions of Hearts in the Scales of Justice!

Mrs. Helen Bergkamp, of Wichita, Kansas, on a visit to Ars, France, in the company of her late husband, was inspired on seeing a statue of Our Lady on which St. John Vianney had placed a locket over Our Lady's Heart in which he placed the names of all his parishioners.

Her brother is the Bishop of Wichita, and the thought came to her: "Oh, if only all the parish priests of the world could place their parishioners in Our Lady's Heart!" So, she had a large statue made with *a recess inside the heart to receive computer discs.* She sent the statue to Fatima to be enshrined in the Queen of the World center at the Fatima Castle. Now there is a movement throughout the world to place *fifty million names in Our Lady's Heart.* A million were pledged from the Philippines alone.

Dr. Mark Miravelle, S.T.D., greeting the Pope on July 31, 1999.

These names will join the millions who have signed the petition for dogma mentioned above which, like the collegial consecration of 1984, will be the sign of a great victory in God's final effort to wrest mankind from the reign of Satan.

Perhaps the Sacred Hearts do not call all lay persons to such degrees of apostleship. But do they not call us all at least to ask our neighbors to place their names in Our Lady's Heart, to be offered to the Sacred Heart of Her Son?

Now, God's final effort, begun in 1673, after more than three hundred years, presents the alternative of "annihilation of several entire nations." And the laity are beginning to realize that the effort must become theirs.

Statue of the Immaculate Heart of Mary at Queen of the World Center at the Fatima Castle. Names placed in the heart of the statue will share in special Masses and in prayers of all others throughout the world, joined in response to conditions of our Lady of Fatima to obtain Her promise: *"My Immaculate Heart will triumph...an era of peace will be granted to mankind."*

CHAPTER TWENTY ONE

FOR EVERYONE

The Lay Apostolate Foundation believes that the examples given in the last chapter are the tip of a lofty mountain peeking above the clouds. Hundreds of lay persons have started evangelizing on the internet. Hundreds more, despite busy and full lives, are vitally involved in parishes and in something as simple as name gathering for consecration to the Sacred Hearts.

A medical doctor in New York recently wrote and published a seven-hundred page book on religions and cults with a loving invitation to all to join the Catholic Church. He had previously written 67 other books and 34 pamphlets. He was president of the Cursillo movement in New York for 40 years, and of the Hispanic Catholic Charismatic Renewal in New York for 25 years.

Does this seem like *a full-time* apostolate?

On the contrary! In 1998, when he produced that 700-page book, he was *still practicing medicine full time* with more than 150,000 patients since 1961.[40]

While many who know of God's final effort do NOTHING to implement it, **the growing response of the laity is now one of great hope.** As we mentioned before, Pope John Paul II hailed this growing response in his millennial encyclical as ***one of the three greatest signs of hope in the Church.***

---

[40] Dr. Jerome Dominguez, M.D., Ph.D., Box 240, New York, NY 10032.

The other two signs of hope seen by the Pope are ecumenism, and acceptance of charisms. The latter also seems especially evident in the laity.

Let us say it again: This is no reflection on the clergy. This is the work of the Holy Spirit, says the Council. This is God's Will *for this third day* of the "week of Fatima," *this time of God's "final effort" to draw mankind from the reign of Satan and establish the reign of His Love.*

This is the time when Our Lord, through His vicar on earth, is saying to the laity of the world: "You, too, go into My vineyard!" You are needed!

Keeping Marthe Robin alive for thirty years solely on His Sacrament of Love, Jesus asked her to make known His Will that the laity become involved even to the degree of making a five-day retreat, saying: "*The laity will renew the Church.*"

The Message of Response

Most important, as we come to the end of this book on the third day of the Fatima week, is the message of *response* **—the message of *what to do.***

The author with Most Rev. John Venancio, Bishop of Fatima.

That message was carefully worded by the Most Rev. John Venancio, the second bishop of Fatima.

We have cited all the above examples of lay involvement today because *that is precisely the message* given by the bishop in this most important apostolic directive of his Fatima episcopate.

For greater appreciation of his message, I would like to declare that I knew this holy bishop intimately. I traveled with him once to Russia, three times around the world, and once around the continent of Africa. In addition to being the Bishop of Fatima, he was one of the holiest and most dedicated persons I have ever known (I believe Bl. Padre Pio would agree). After his retirement, we saw him frequently kneeling at Fatima in the chapel of the apparitions in prayer. He had taught theology at a major seminary in Rome before he became bishop of Fatima. Our Lady of Fatima had chosen as Her bishop a prelate of great learning (fluent in several languages) and of Holiness.

Written on the tomb of his predecessor in the Basilica of Fatima is the simple inscription: "Here lies *the Bishop of Our Lady*." On Bishop Venancio's tomb could be written: "Here lies *the Bishop of the Queen of the World*."

In this major "encyclical" of his episcopate, he says that *no matter who we are or what may be our state of life*, we are ALL called to respond to the requests of the Sacred Hearts.

The Bishop Explains

Following are a few excerpts adapted from that message which appears in its entirety at the end of my book *Dear Bishop!*.

Please read them *as words from Our Lady of Fatima Herself*.

"There are millions of people who have never felt called to an apostolate.

"For instance, there are the great number of children, old people, invalids, plus millions of parents absorbed exclusively from morning to night in household chores, the care of their children, or their work in fields or factory, without either the time or the possibility of intense involvement in the apostolate.

"Our Lady, who came to the children of Fatima, calls them all.

"It can be, and it is, the great and important task of the Blue Army of Our Lady of Fatima (the World Apostolate of Fatima) to mobilize these vast reserves of the faithful and bring them into conscientious service of the Church, to collaborate with other movements and *to give new life to the various forms of apostolic activity.*

"*All the persons* mentioned above (children, old people, invalids, parents), even if they may suffer some physical of psychological problems, *can respond to the requests made by the Queen of the Rosary.*

"They can pray, they can make sacrifices, they can expiate, they can live and work according to the desires of the Immaculate Heart of Mary. Thus they will fulfill the essential part of the sprit of the message, the great work to which we all are called: *the interior renovation of the Church.*

Nothing New

The bishop quotes at some length from the encyclical of Pius XI on Atheistic Communism, which says: "*There are too many who fulfill more or less faithfully the more essential obligations of the religion they boast of professing, but have no desire of knowing it better or deepening their inward conviction... In these days when the winds of strife and persecution blow so fiercely, they will be swept away defenseless in this new deluge which threatens the world.*"

Following the words of the Pope, the bishop continues:

"An attraction of the Blue Army (the message of Fatima) is that it asks nothing new. The old devotional practices of the Church, carried out with greater fervor of spirit, will suffice.

"The task of the Blue Army of Our Lady of Fatima consists in making known to the whole world the

Message of Fatima by all the means at its disposal **so that men of all nations will make it real in their personal lives.**

"If anyone asks, 'Why the Blue Army?,' we ask in return: 'Why did Our Lady come to Fatima with these requests (which are fulfilled in the Blue Army pledge)?'

"Why? Because men so often turn a deaf ear to the voice of the Church. So, *God sends His Immaculate Mother to remind men in an extraordinary manner of these obligations.*

A Call to ALL

"At the same time, God is reminding the Church. (Pope John Paul II said: "The message of Fatima in a certain way *compels* the Church.")

"The message of Fatima is addressed to all men without exception, regardless of any ecclesiastical organization. So the Blue Army is addressed to all, and is open to all.

"To be already a member of any Marian association does not justify a refusal to join the Blue Army. This is not a movement apart from others. In harmony with the message of Fatima, it seeks to bring every individual to pray more than they ever did before, to do penance for the sins of the world, and to consecrate themselves to the Immaculate Heart of Mary.

"It follows that each and every form of the Apostolate of the laity, animated by this spiritual renewal for which Our Lady came at Fatima, will reap inestimable profit in personal sanctification of the individual and of the entire apostolate.

Special Call to Marian Devotees

"It would be a lamentable error to see in the Blue Army nothing more than a tributary stream to other Marian movements. Not at all. These Marian movements should be the first to seek to understand and to fulfill the message of the Queen of Heaven. They should form the vanguard of the Army of the 'Conqueror in all the battles of God.'

"The Blue Army of Our Lady of Fatima calls to each and all, great and small, rich and poor, cultured and ignorant. In this combat, every man of good will is engaged. And peace belongs to those who are united in the fight.

"We have arrived at a very definite crossroads in the history of the world. The future hangs in the balance. The powers of darkness, in an apocalyptic effort, advance in united strength to try to blot out the name of God from the entire world.

"It is into this battle that Our Lady comes, having appeared at Fatima to bring us Her message from Heaven, to place in our hands the arms of victory."

Bl. Padre Pio, when asked if it was a good thing to join the Blue Army, answered: *"Could you do anything better?"* Above: The author serving Bl. Padre Pio's Mass.

Chapter Twenty Two

FOUR DIVISIONS

This holy "Bishop of the Queen of the World" is saying that all—every single person including even small children!—are being asked by Our Lady to offer themselves to the Heart of Jesus, through Her Immaculate Heart, to draw men from the reign of Satan and to destroy that reign.

It is interesting that MOST of the lay apostles we have encountered had their beginning, or were at least a part of, the Blue Army—that army of which the first Cardinal of the Church under three Popes (Cardinal Tisserant) said:

"Does not the Queen need Her army to win the battle against Satan?"

It is a massive battle. It is apocalyptic. It calls for a universal response. And we will all be held responsible if we do not respond.

Our Lady said at Akita that if we do not act, and a chastisement "worse than the deluge" must come, "the GOOD will be destroyed with the bad."

The good people (Pius XI described them as "more or less faithful") will deserve it because they are the ones who did not prevent it. The Pope (as quoted above by Our Lady's Bishop) said: "The Catholic who does not live *really and sincerely* according to the Faith he professes will not long be master of himself in these days when the winds of strife and persecution blow so fiercely, and *will be swept away defenseless in this new deluge which threatens the world.*" (From the encyclical on Atheistic Communism.)

A Diversified Army of Response

Since Pope Pius XI said this solemnly in an encyclical to all the bishops and faithful of the world, the better part of a century has passed, including eighty years of widespread lack of adequate response to the Fatima message.

In the short time we may have left for an adequate response, is there much hope that we will touch the hearts of most Catholics?

If we answer realistically that there is not much hope, then what else can we do? The Sacred Hearts have told us. We can persuade those who know *to form an elite corps* to make up in quality (spiritual fighting skill) what may be lacking in quantity.

As a well-diversified army, we can attack the enemy on different levels. We can back up the first division of those thousands who are willing to take the first step of consecration to the Sacred Hearts *with three other divisions, one stronger than the other!*

The First Division

The first and biggest division is put in the field simply by an act of consecration. We recruit them just by asking: "Would you like to put your name in Our Lady's Heart?" And get them to sign their name for that purpose.

The next stronger force is made of those who pledge to wear the Scapular as a sign of that consecration, with the Morning Offering enforced by daily recitation of the Rosary. This division alone, if in sufficient number, would gain the field. They have already, in fulfillment of the prophecy of Bl. Padre Pio, obtained the "miraculous" change in Russia and brought us into the third day.

"Sufficient Number"

We have been encouraged to believe in a "sufficient number" by the prophecy of Bl. Padre Pio, who said: "Russia will be converted when there is a Blue Army member for every Communist." Some twenty-five million have made the Blue Army pledge, and another million were added in the Philippines the very year before the collegial consecration.

The Communists (who personified the forces of militant atheism) had been diminishing while Our Lady's Army was moving, however slowly, ahead. In 1984, the collegial consecration was made and the cold war ended.

We asked Sister Lucia if this meant that the world would now avoid the "annihilation of nations" of which Our Lady spoke at Fatima. She said the consecration would have its effect, "*but the Blue Army will have much to do.*" She revealed that due to the consecration, atomic war was avoided in 1985.

That is also when she said: "The Fatima week has just begun...we are in the third day."

The Third Division

Now is the time when Our Lady's spiritual army has "much" to do. And it is necessary to call up that special third division of *Communions of Reparation.*

Many Catholics have already made Communions of Reparation on nine consecutive First Fridays. Now they are asked to make them on First Saturdays. Already in a previous chapter, we have explained the importance and urgency of the First Saturdays. If Bl. Padre Pio could predict the change in Russia when a sufficient number were fulfilling the Fatima (Blue Army) pledge, can we not say now that the tidal wave of evil will be turned back when there are sufficient First Saturday Communions of Reparation?

Unfortunately, after more than half a century, despite the example set by the Pope and despite all other efforts, few are making the First Saturdays. Many (often even priests) seem not even to know about them.

Elizabeth Szanto, to whom Our Lady revealed the message of Her Flame of Love, asked: "Why don't you perform miracles so people believe you, as you did at Fatima?" Our Lady answered sadly:

"My daughter, even if I were to perform great miracles, people would not believe. I asked for the First Saturdays and who paid any attention to My requests?"[41]

And Our Lady was shedding tears.

It is time to add the fourth division, the elite corps!

The Elite Corps

The ultimate fighting division, as we have said, is made up of those who make *the Vigils of the Two Hearts,* beginning with Mass of the Sacred Heart on the evening of the First Friday and spending several hours with the Eucharistic Heart of Jesus in the exposed Blessed Sacrament, concluding with Mass of the Immaculate Heart and the second Communion of Reparation on First Saturday morning.

This fourth division of Our Lady's spiritual army (adding First Friday/Saturday vigils to basic pledge) can *quickly* obtain the victory *if pursued vigorously even by the few who may read this book.*

We have already spoken at some length of the First Saturdays with a mention of the vigils. Let us add a few more words about the vigilers.

On the Calvary of Lourdes

After coming upon an English all-night vigil group in Fatima in 1956, and then three years later running into them at 2:00 in the morning with their arms outstretched before the grotto of Lourdes, I was convinced that HERE was the final heroic practice of the prayer and sacrifice which could change the course of history. Here was what might ultimately balance the scales of Divine Justice. Here was the ultimate response to the requests of the Sacred Hearts.

Ten years later, after having myself made many vigils, it was in the chapel at Paray-le-Monial (where Our Lord revealed His Sacred Heart to St. Margaret Mary) that I felt inspired to write a book about it.

That book, *Night of Love*, became so much in demand that when the last printing was exhausted, many people made photocopies. Others repaired their copies with tape and used them almost to the point of disintegration. Over and over, I received appeals for a new printing. But I felt there was more of this message to come.

---

[41] The writings of Elizabeth Szanto were approved by the local bishop and have subsequently been published in 17 languages. See *Her Glorious Title*, pg. 118.

Then, in 1992, I received a letter from the housekeeper of a 91 year old priest who wrote:

"Dear Mr. Haffert: You do not know me but I feel I know you. For 58 years, I have been keeping house for Fr. Herman Dietz. Many years ago we ordered two copies of *Night of Love* which we have been using for Holy Hours ever since.

"Making it Daily"

"Last month, I forgot to bring the books home with me from church. Early next morning I went over before anyone came, but the books were gone. So I am writing for a special favor. Could you send us two more?"

To my surprise, a few days later a letter came from the 91 year old priest himself. In shaky hand, he wrote: "I have used this wonderful book for many years. Recently, after making a First Saturday Holy Hour, I left it in the church. Someone took it. It is so good. I suppose whoever took it liked it and kept it. *I am 91 and too old to make an all–night vigil, so I make only a Holy Hour* **and make it daily.**"

When we finally published a new edition I quoted these two letters and marveled at all the power of the prayer of that holy old priest and his housekeeper who, no longer able to make vigils, were making up the time with holy hours and Communions of Reparation *every day.*

Finally, in 1997, we produced an improved edition in witness to the growth of the First Friday-Saturday Communions of Reparation around the world—adding the beautiful revelations of God the Father made known only in recent years.

We could see the *unfolding* of the devotion of the Two Hearts glowing on the horizon. We could rejoice in hope with Sister Lucia: "The triumph is an *ongoing process.*" Were not the increasing number of First Friday/Saturday vigils a sign of the ultimate success of God's effort to wrest mankind from the reign of Satan through the flaming love of the Sacred Hearts?

CHAPTER TWENTY THREE

ADDED FORCE

S t. Grignion de Montfort, who foresaw the whole "unfolding" of devotion to the Two Hearts, was born in 1673, at the very time the Sacred Heart was appearing to St. Margaret Mary. He wrote prophetically:

"If the falsely enlightened, whom the devil has so miserably misled even in prayer, had known how to find Mary, and through Her to find Jesus, and through Jesus, God the Father, they would not have had such terrible falls."

That is the "on-going process" which began in force at Paray le Monial, picked up force at Fatima, and has brought us into the third day, when "the Blue Army will have much to do." St. Grignion continues: "The saints tell us that when we have once found Mary, and through Mary, Jesus, and through Jesus, God the Father, we have found all good."

We will then have come into the era of the Divine Will, already dawning in many souls at the present moment.

Double the Force

"He who says *all*," St. Grignion continues, "leaves out nothing. Our spiritual journey *is a dynamic process* which takes us through Mary to Jesus, in union with the Holy Spirit, back home to God Our Father."

But even for many of the best of us, the process is not dynamic. The words "through Mary to Jesus" are more an expression than a reality. Many say the words and believe them, but do not experience their dynamism.

Here is where the force of our response to the Two Hearts could be doubled. Yes, and far more! It could be made almost infinitely more powerful. But how can we describe this dynamism? How can we explain the difference between saying prayers and really praying? And if we should succeed in describing it, how can we make it personally real in ourselves?

Let us fervently ask the Holy Spirit for light. Let us join at this very moment in saying:

"Lord Jesus, Son of God our Father, coming as Our Lady of All Nations, Your Mother has taught us to ask you to send NOW Your Holy Spirit over the earth. Send Him now to us that we may understand and, understanding, to increase our effectiveness for the triumph of Your Sacred Heart through the Immaculate Heart of our Mother."

Focus

Recently, a comparison came to light which might be a great help. It is called the "Magic Eye." It is a computer-generated picture called a stereogram which is perfectly flat. But if you "focus" properly a three dimensional picture will emerge.[42]

Indeed, it will not only emerge, but you will find yourself gazing into it almost as though you were "entering in" what you are seeing.

At first, you see only a maze of colored dots or things which have no meaning. But when you focus "through" the flat image you are suddenly in the third dimension.

This is what should happen when we pray. We should focus into the new dimension of the supernatural. But many of us are not getting beyond the flat picture.

How It Feels

When we become *aware* that we are communicating with God or the Saints, we cross the chasm between belief and realization. Although in this world, we become at the same time in *the more real world of God*. It is as radical an

---

[42] There are several websites with samples of stereograms including *Magic Eye* at www.magiceye.com.

experience as looking at a flat and meaningless surface and suddenly being in the third dimension.

How much more meaningful and powerful our prayer becomes when we are *aware* that GOD is there—GOD is LISTENING.

Yet many pray thousands of words and never cross the chasm into that wonderful, love-filled supernatural world.

We were surprised to discover at one of our Lay Apostles retreats that many of those present had never really crossed that chasm, even though they had been daily communicants for many years, and even though for some it was their fourth annual Lay Apostles retreat.

How To Cross

This led to an exchange on a level we had never before experienced. We began to speak of our personal prayer experience. We found that at least one of the group was "in focus" most of the time. She had for some years developed into living in the Divine Will. Some others had *never* focused. Others found that they were triggered into the supernatural dimension just by saying "Jesus." Most said it happened rarely, and seemed like some special grace of the moment.

Perhaps the reader can recall one of those moments of special awareness. Perhaps it was at a Shrine, in a Charismatic meeting, touching the rock of Lourdes, or at the chapel of the apparitions in Fatima. And perhaps we thought this was just special, and not something we should experience every time we pray.

But it is something we should expect every time we pray!

If we do not, there is one special reason: We have not fully surrendered ourselves to God.

Take It Away!

Once a man was in the rain at the grotto in Lourdes without a coat. He knew he would become wet, but he wanted to attend Mass in this holy place.

After some time, he wondered that although it was raining very heavily, he did not feel wet. He reached his hand under the thin jacket he was wearing. The rain did not seem to have gone through. He was dry. Two thoughts came to him: 1) Maybe the thin garment was somehow waterproof; 2) Maybe this was a "funny kind" of rain.

Miracle? The supernatural happening to *him*? No such thought.

After Mass, he started to walk across the esplanade which, in the heavy rain, was completely covered with water which could not escape from the asphalt fast enough. Suddenly, his foot went into a declivity in water over his shoe.

Instinctively, he bent over and removed his shoe to empty out the water.

But his foot was dry.

It *was* a miracle!

In that moment of realization did he cry out in thanksgiving? Did he welcome this evidence of a touch of kindness from His Creator? No. He cried out: "All right! I believe, Lord. Now let me get wet!"

He hesitated to cross the chasm between belief in the supernatural and its reality. It felt too much like giving up one world for another. It was like, going swimming for the first time, being afraid to take one's feet off the bottom.

"Yes"

But the refusal to acknowledge God's intimacy lasted but a moment. It was almost at once replaced with an awesome "Thank you." It was replaced with "Yes."

He walked in the rain for another two hours in wonder, in "focus."

Since I do not know what experiences others may have, I hope the sharing of my own experiences may be helpful. For me, there are two simple things which I find bring me into focus as much as that miracle in the rain: the Rosary and the Scapular.

I think this is true also for many, as for St. Claude de la Colombiere. It is the realization when praying the Rosary while clothed in Our Lady's mantle that She is there. She is listening. And more than just aware that She is listening, I feel myself *aware* in Her presence. Bathed in the light of Her Heart, I am in that deep dimension of the supernatural.

Easy to Lose

This is what happened to the children of Fatima. Our Lady bathed them in the light of Her heart after they said "Yes." And suddenly, as Lucia describes it: "*We felt lost in God.*" And they had an *awareness* of God in the Eucharist.

That is the great wonder of it. It becomes difficult to put into words. It is much like the stereogram.

When you succeed in focusing on the three dimensions of a stereogram, you find that you can look all around in it, from one detail to another. You can become lost in it.

But it takes focus—which is comparable to our "Yes" to crossing the chasm to the supernatural. And the moment you start thinking of something else, you lose it as happens with the stereogram. The moment you look *at the picture itself*, you see nothing but colored dots.

Takes Practice

There are three suggested ways to "see through" a stereogram. One of them is to hold the image very close to the eyes, and then slowly move it away while trying not to look at the picture itself but, as it were, *through* it.

Some try over and over before getting into focus. Others focus quickly. But after it happens, the more one practices the more easily and quickly one can enter the three dimensions.

The same is true of prayer. Once we have said "Yes," trusting our minds and hearts to let go and enter the infinite world, we can focus into that wonderful awareness which makes prayers not just words but something one cannot put into words.

Can we imagine what it would mean if all of who attended daily Mass, all who practiced devotions like the Rosary and the First Saturdays and vigils were in *focus*? Can we imagine how much the third day would be shortened!

CHAPTER TWENTY FOUR

CONCLUSION

Some of the chapters in this book might have been, and perhaps should have been, as long as the book itself. The 1993 statement of Sister Lucia, which has been divided and scattered throughout these chapters, perhaps leaves as many questions as we have given answers.

We see that the triumph is indeed an ongoing process from the time St. John the Evangelist spoke to St. Gertrude, in 1292, of devotion to the Sacred Heart to the time of the revelation of the Sacred Heart to St. Margaret Mary in 1673 (the century of St. John Eudes and St. Grignion de Montfort), to the medal of the Two Hearts revealed to St. Catherine Labouré, followed by Pontmain and Pellevoisin (where Our Lady showed the Scapular as a sign of the Two Hearts) from 1830 to 1871. Finally at Fatima, from 1917 to 2000 (with Sister Lucia still kept in the world as God's messenger), we see more clearly the final appeal of the Love of God to save man from himself, to deliver him from Satan, and to destroy Satan's reign in the world.

Now we face the ultimate alternative: atomic war.

What To DO

The one lesson we should have learned is that *it all depends on our response.* The bishops of the world are to promote the devotion of the Two Hearts, the Communions of Reparation. The laity are to take the initiative.

Every man, woman, and child is called. ALL can place their names in Our Lady's Heart. At an international center in the castle of Fatima, an image of Our Lady awaits with a recess beneath Her Heart to receive them, even in countless millions.[43]

The name-gatherers distribute a picture of this statue with the prayer of Our Lady of All Nations, which Our Lady requested to speed the triumph She has promised. We are given to believe that the triumph will actually begin when enough persons have given their hearts and are saying this prayer:

"Lord Jesus Christ, Son of the Eternal Father, send now Your Holy Spirit over the earth. Let the Holy Spirit live in the hearts of all peoples to save them from degeneration, disaster, and war. May Our Lady of All Nations, who once was Mary,[44] be our advocate!"

The Second Division

Even more urgently, we are asked, after giving our hearts, to make, and get others to make, the Fatima pledge:

"Dear Mother, who promised at Fatima to convert Russia and to bring peace to all mankind, in reparation for my sins and the sins of the whole world, I solemnly promise to your Immaculate Heart:

"1) To offer up every day the sacrifices demanded by my daily duty;

"2) To pray part of the Rosary (five decades) daily while thinking of the mysteries;

"3) To wear the Scapular of Mount Carmel as profession of this promise and as an act of consecration to you. I shall renew this promise often, especially in moments of temptation."[45]

---

[43] To place your name in the Immaculate Heart of Mary at the castle in Fatima, write: *Sedes Mundi Reginae*, Ao Castelo, Ourem, Portugal. In the U.S.: Queen of the World Center, PO Box 20870, Wichita, KS 67208. Also, online at www.101foundation.com, or email immaculateheart@101foundation.com

[44] Until this time when "God has entrusted the peace of the world to Her" (Bl. Jacinta), we have thought of Our Lady as the silent Woman of the Scriptures. Now She comes in power, as the Lady of All Nations, to crush the head of Satan.

We fulfill this pledge by living the following prayer:

The Morning Offering

"O Most Holy Trinity, in union with the Immaculate Heart of Mary (*here kiss the Scapular*), I offer Thee every thought, word, action, pain and suffering of this day, together with the Precious Blood of Jesus from all the altars throughout the world, in reparation for my sins and the sins of the world.

"O My Jesus, I desire to gain every indulgence and merit I can this day and I offer them, together with myself, to the Immaculate Heart of Mary, Mediatrix of all Your Grace, that She may best apply them to the interests of Your Most Sacred Heart.

"Sacred Heart of Jesus, have mercy on us! Precious Blood of Jesus, save us! Immaculate Heart of Mary, pray for us! Amen."

The Powerful Divisions

The first two divisions (those who give their names and those who make the pledge) might eventually be of sufficient number to bring about the triumph. But "eventually" might be after a chastisement worse than the deluge.

We need special divisions. *We need those special souls, because of whom Our Lady said at Akita: "SO FAR I have been able to hold back the chastisement."*

It lies in the power *of each one of us* to give Our Lady that elite corps.

Anyone can make the First Saturday devotion on his own. And, we can ask our pastors to have the First Saturday devotion in our parish. We can join, or form, a group to help conduct it, and to get parishioners to attend.

If approached in the right manner (not "commanding" but offering to help), most pastors will welcome this initiative. It can begin first with having the Rosary before or after Mass. Then, it is an easy step to the First Saturdays.

---

45 This pledge does not bind under pain of sin but indicates a sincere resolve to fulfill these basic requests of Our Lady, as set forth by Sister Lucia and the first Bishop of Fatima. Pledges may be sent to the international center of the Blue Army at Fatima or to national or local centers to share in the spiritual benefits. The U.S. center is: Blue Army Shrine, Washington, NJ 07882.

In extreme cases, if the pastor does not respond after sincere and repeated efforts, we should write to the bishop.

Once the First Saturday devotion is established, the same First Saturday group can "move up" to First Friday/Saturday vigils.

Most likely there is already a vigil within easy distance from where you live. If so, begin there! Once you have made a vigil you will be a part of the truly powerful division of Our Lady's Army. You will be in the front line of the battle for the triumph of the Sacred Hearts. And your personal rewards will be great beyond imagining.

It is no longer a time to say, "It is up to them." It is time to say, "It is up to me."

Close-up of the heart of the statue at the Queen of the World Center at the Fatima castle in which names will be placed on a computer disk. The prayer on the heart reads: "*Holy Mary Mother of the universe, pray for us. Hold us forever in the protection of your maternal heart until we are safe in paradise.*"

FOUR STEPS TO THE TRIUMPH OF THE SACRED HEARTS

The first step is the apostolate of worldwide consecration: The gathering of millions of names into the refuge of the Immaculate Heart of Mary for the triumph of the Sacred Heart of Her Son.

The names are actually placed in the heart of Her statue at the museum-center of the Queen of the World at Fatima.

This is an apostolate of consecration to the Immaculate Heart of Mary with a timely and urgent incentive: To give millions of hearts to Jesus, through the Flame of Love of His Mother's own heart, in the new millennium.

Contact
Queen of the World Center
PO Box 20870
Wichita, KS 67208

The second step is the basic Fatima pledge. The third step is the First Saturday devotion. The fourth step includes prayer cells and First Friday/Saturday vigils.

These steps are being taken in many apostolates, among which the Blue Army (World Apostolate of Fatima) is especially recognized.

Contact
The Blue Army
PO Box 976
Washington, NJ 07882